the
Heart
of the
Akashic Records
Revealed

Works Published

How to Read the Akashic Records (2009, Sounds True)

Healing Through the Akashic Records (2011, Sounds True)

*Discover Your Soul's Path Through
the Akashic Records* (2015, Hay House)

*Inspired Manifesting: Elevate Your Energy and Ignite Your Dreams
Through the Akashic Records* (2020, Energy Integrity)

the

Heart
of the
Akashic Records
Revealed

A COMPREHENSIVE GUIDE
TO THE TEACHINGS OF THE
PATHWAY PRAYER PROCESS

Dr. Linda Howe

modern wisdom
P R E S S

modern wisdom
P R E S S

Modern Wisdom Press
Boulder, Colorado, USA
www.modernwisdompress.com

Published 2022
Cover and interior design: KP Design
Author photo: Garen Hudson

DISCLAIMER
Neither the author nor the publisher assume any responsibility for errors,
omissions, or contrary interpretations of the subject matter within.

MEDICAL DISCLAIMER
The information in this book is a result of years of practical experience
by the author. This information is not intended as a substitute for the
advice provided by your physician or other healthcare professional. Do
not use the information in this book for diagnosing or treating a health
problem or disease, or prescribing medication or other treatment.

I dedicate this work of my lifetime to you, my beloved students. Teaching this work to thousands of students around the world for the past three decades has infused me with a quality of aliveness I dreamt about as a little girl. Teaching is one of the great joys of my life, igniting the Light within me, my students, and the work itself. Students, thank you for sharing your curiosity, meaningful questions, and desire to know more, be better, and do greater things today than yesterday. May you know yourselves as one—with an open Mind, a warm Heart, and a resilient Will.

TABLE OF CONTENTS

INTRODUCTION

a·ka·sha /*ə'käSHə*/

When I first heard the word "**AKASHA**": *AAH-KAA-SHAA*, sound vibrations resonated through my heart in unique ways. I was moved—riveted even—and felt compelled to know more. It was 1994 when I made my first conscious, deliberate excursion into the Akashic Records. Having heard that this realm was "exclusive," solely for mystics, scholars, and saints, I did not think it was open to everyday spiritual seekers like me. And yet, I was undeniably captivated by the irresistible sound of the word: *Aah-kaa-shaa.*

In the beginning, I experienced the Akasha as a mysterious, mystical dimension—a cosmic library of sorts—marked by random energies and celestial sounds. Having been sorely disappointed by religions and other spiritual systems, my expectation for a beneficial relationship with the Akasha was low. Yet, surprisingly, this Field has been irresistible, empowering the transformation I craved: from painful limitations to practical expressions of the treasures of my Innermost Self. With delight, I discovered that the Akasha was more potent than a cosmic light bath, more inspiring than any other sacred space I had encountered, and embedded with spiritual wisdom that is helpful in daily life. Along the way, Akashic Light has become central to my journey.

Beckoned and drawn to this space repeatedly over the past three decades, I have discovered an unlimited treasure trove of insights, guidance, and wisdom applicable to everyday life. I've come to know the Akashic Records as a remarkable spiritual resource for personal development and useful inspiration, a dimension informed with the consciousness of unconditional love for individuals and all creation.

Having taught tens of thousands of students around the globe and published four books about the Akasha, it is now my specialty—and I love sharing it! For years, Practitioners have requested that the core of the work be accessible in one compilation, which is why you are now holding this entire curriculum in your hands. This book contains the full range of the work revealed to me from the Heart of the Records via the Pathway Prayer Process.

However, it does not pretend, nor do I intend to answer, every possible question about this infinite realm, the Akasha. As you move through this material, questions may arise about things not addressed here (such as "What is Soul and where does it originate?" or "What is the nature of the Ultimate Reality?"). It is impossible to capture everything. Worry not! Your next step on the journey will still be illuminated without every question answered. And there is power in holding powerful questions that are not easily answered. Every time you meet this work, there is more to discover. This work is alive and expansive.

And now for a bold but true statement: This work is ideal for everyone! Whether you are completely new to the Path or a seasoned veteran of Akashic explorations, you'll find something here to fuel your journey. You can use this volume as a companion to the Akashic Records classes I've developed or pursue it independently for your own edification and enlightenment. Doing this work will empower and guide you to become a solid Akashic Records Reader for yourself and one well prepared to assist others along their way. Please note, though, that while this work can bring you to new levels of excellence, it is *not* the same as obtaining a recognized Certification earned by studying with me or one of my recognized Certified Teachers. (You can explore possibilities to become certified on my website: www.lindahowe.com /classes-with-linda-howe/.)

Engaging with this material to the best of your ability—whether you jump into the middle, dive into the depths of the final sections, or deliberately wade into the beginning—will propel you to your next level of evolution. There is no wrong way to use this material! Experiment, experience, and enjoy! This work will meet you wherever you are. Your quest for transformation is your starting point. Do what you can, as you are able, based on what inspires you in any given moment, and you'll find yourself in an ever-expanding reality. By giving yourself a chance, you are certain to grow.

Ultimately, working in the heart of the Akasha is a resource for steering us away from old ideas into greater possibilities so we can become the people we know we are here to be. There is more than enough here for a lifetime. So, take your time moving through this material. You are who you are meant to be, and *now* is the most marvelous time in all of your lifetimes.

Enjoy!

HOW TO USE THIS GUIDE

Welcome to your Amazing Akashic Adventure! I am so glad that you chose to join tens of thousands of spiritual seekers worldwide. This Guide contains all of my certified teaching materials, condensing into one comprehensive curriculum a wide range of information, teachings, best practices, meditations, and practical exercises designed to bring you into the deep waters of the Akashic Records. One empowering exercise at a time, we will examine and explore each subject and see how it applies to your daily life—whether you are hearing "Akasha" for the first time, a new student to my work, a longtime Practitioner, or a seasoned Certified Teacher.

Ours is the Age of Awakening Spiritual Awareness—and it's a time like no other. It is characterized by a shift in collective consciousness, which is accomplished one Soul at a time. We have all chosen to be on Earth for this remarkable transformation. To succeed in our spiritual mission, we need effective spiritual resources. The Akashic Records are precisely that: an infinite spiritual resource for our transformation, useful in these times of profound growth, ideally suited for our challenge. The Records will help us sense where we are as individuals and as a species so we can address the opportunities at hand.

There are many changes in our perceptions in our new era, beginning with our identity. Historically, we have defined ourselves by our families, cultural or religious groups, and even political affiliations. That is all changing. Now, we are free to stand with others—beyond bloodline and geographical boundaries—with whom we share beliefs, values, and perspectives on Life. As a result, we are internally, personally determined instead of being externally identified by others.

Working in the Akashic Records is an ideal resource for these times and accessible to so many because this is a spiritual resource—decidedly nonreligious and not aligned with any dogma or institution. Some important elements of the Shift we are undergoing live in the distinctions we are now making, such as spiritual maturity rather than immaturity; the reality of our Oneness as opposed to the illusion of separation; and personal responsibility instead of blame. Essentially, humanity is shifting from a perception of the human self as a dismal, damaged-at-the-core, unenlightened sinner to awareness of our immutable goodness, Infinite Light, and Divine Power at the center of our being.

Spiritual practice in the Akashic Records is a sacred opportunity. And so the following Ground Rules have been developed over time to support harmonious relations, dignifying all individuals involved. Your awareness of and adherence to these Ground Rules nurtures your spiritual maturity and contributes to a culture of kindness and respect, blessing us all. Together, let's honor the wisdom, compassion, and honorable engagement of everyone inspired to participate in this work.

1 Let yourself be a student in this class. You
   deserve to learn all you can.

2 This is not a generic teaching about the Akashic Records,
   but rather a specific method using the Pathway Prayer
   Process to Access the Heart of the Akashic Records©.

3 Refrain from using other systems or techniques while learning this new method. While you may be an expert in another discipline, please give yourself a fair chance to learn this method with a beginner's mind.

This Guide is presented in three distinct segments:

- *Level I:* How to Read the Akashic Records. We begin with the method and foundational principles so that you can gain a more conscious connection with your Soul using the Pathway Prayer Process to Access the Heart of the Akashic Records. Our focus is on exploring the Akashic Records and their potential and promises for your growth and transformation. Fundamental concepts supporting your success in the Records are presented, including the Akashic Absolutes and the Akashic approach to spiritual work for personal transformation. (Recommended companion reading for this Level: *How to Read the Akashic Records.*)

- *Level II:* Healing Through the Akashic Records. With a solid foundation in place, you will continue to increase your under-standing of healing work in the Akashic Records by exploring and experiencing practices to strengthen yourself as an Akashic Records Practitioner. Here are many ways of delving into your issues for resolution—setting standards and making it easier for you to become increasingly proficient in your practice, thereby developing your ability to do remarkable, effective, transformational work with others. Our intent in this section is personal healing and transformation, making peace with yourself and others, finding greater freedom from limiting patterns, and refining your effective work with others. Here we explore basic protocols for Clearing Unwanted Ancestral Patterns, Reconciling Past Lives, and Energy Healing in the Records. Naturally, we examine the Akashic perspective on Karma and learn how to be free from unfavorable Karmic pat-terns. Also included are Guided Meditations and Empowerment Exercises. Our focus is on our own healing first and then on working with others, based on the principle that we can only transmit what we have experienced. There is no reason to be shy; practice is the Path. (Recommended companion reading for this Level: *Healing Through the Akashic Records.*)

• And then comes *Level III:* Manifesting Your Soul's Purposes. Expand your awareness, experience, expression, and enjoyment of your Soul's Purposes in this lifetime! Here is your opportunity to recognize your unique usefulness in the world, see the value of your contributions, and resolve obstacles to powerful self-expression. Since this is the lifetime to bring your Soul's Purposes to life, this work will propel you in that direction. Essential understandings from the Records about the nature of the Soul, its purposes, and the relationship of your Soul's Purposes to your Destiny will be examined, followed by spiritual interpretations of prosperity, abundance, money, obstacles, obstructions, and even self-sabotage. Discover conditions that support your prosperity and make peace with decisions in other lifetimes still affecting you now. (Recommended companion reading for this Level: *Discover Your Soul's Path Through the Akashic Records* and *Inspired Manifesting: Elevate Your Energy and Ignite Your Dreams Through the Akashic Records!*)

Relax, as I'll share everything you need to know as we go along. As you move through each lesson in this Guide, please do so at the speed of your Soul, making time and space for working in the Records, reflecting, journaling, and mining your experiences for insight, guidance, and wisdom. The material in each Level builds upon the others, often repeating and reinforcing prior concepts. Stay with it as we proceed one step at a time. Ultimately, this is about your co-creative connection with your spiritual authority. Since infinite Truth lives within you, this is a reminder and a remembering. Together we will carve out a safe space and illuminate a well-defined Path so you can shed old ideas of who you are and grow into the magnificent Truth of who you have always been. Your success is assured; you were led to this work by an inner prompting of your Soul because *now is your time*, and you have the natural ability to succeed. *Enjoy!*

SPECIAL TERMINOLOGY

These unique terms are **bolded** when they first appear in the text and defined here to give you a brief introduction before you begin.

Akasha A Sanskrit word meaning "primary substance—that from which all things are formed." This primal energy is the raw material of Life.

Akashic Destiny Seeds held within us as dreams, purposes, and possibilities, which are fulfilled through time and within space using the raw material of Life; the natural, inevitable consequence of manifesting our Soul's Purposes.

Akashic Energy Being in the presence of the Akasha, often experienced as unconditional love.

Akashic Field The convergence of Universal Heart, Mind, and Will.

Akashic Light Your infinitely powerful, always-present, and loving companion that offers insights and guidance to activate the treasure of wisdom embedded in your Soul over lifetimes.

Akashic Manifesting   Making evident something that is inspired by Akashic Light and Wisdom, and making it tangible for the highest good of all.

Akashic Realm   A unified field of consciousness where the Records are accessed and Heart, Mind, and Will are integrated so we can operate as fully synthesized beings.

Akashic Records   A treasury of wisdom, insights, and Truths, accumulated over countless incarnations, inspiring and empowering us to use our human faculties for their highest potential; a dimension of Light; the Records are not an oracle for divination or a deity to be worshipped.

Akashic Records Practitioner   One who is in a conscious, dynamic partnership within the Akashic Realm to enhance their experience of the human journey.

Empowerment Exercises   A series of practices, directions, and inquiries to be taken into your Akashic Records to empower you.

MTLOs   An abbreviation for "Masters, Teachers, and Loved Ones," our guides in the Akashic Records.

Zone of Choice   That inner Akashic Realm we visit in between incarnations to review the progress of our Soul's journey as humans and make selections in partnership with our MTLOs to support our awakening.

MY JOURNEY

One of the first ideas we recognize about the Records is that they are a collection of the stories of the lifetimes we live through, in which we awaken to the Truth of our Divine essence and live that Truth while still human. This idea helps us comprehend the spiritual significance of our life stories; the Akashic Record is the story of your Soul's journey as human. Your story in this lifetime is directly related to your Soul's journey; it is the human expression of your Soul. We recognize a relationship between ordinary life events and your spiritual awakening and subsequent evolution. Please contemplate your story as I share a brief story of my journey to the Records. Upon reflection, there seem to be two stories happening simultaneously: the first about ordinary, everyday human growth and development, and the second, an extraordinary, spiritual awakening.

My upbringing was typical to any Midwestern American girl, grounded in the thought that I would be granted happiness if I managed it well. At the age of 24, after some worldly achievement, I was astonished to find myself unhappy. All the external rewards of Life were mine, including a great job, a wonderful apartment, a car, terrific friends, and the rest. This left me feeling empty inside, prompting my desperate prayer to a God I was not sure existed.

Help came within a few weeks in the form of a moment of life-changing spiritual awareness. I was overcome with feeling known and loved by Life: I was good enough, belonged here, and all would be well. It was tremendous. Nothing in my life prepared me for such a moment. I had done nothing to earn or deserve this, yet it came to me anyway. And so I decided that, whatever that awareness was, I would seek, find, and have it in my life every day. With that, I set out on a quest. From ages 24 to 40, I explored every possible spiritual path available in a valiant effort to recreate the experience I had at 24. It was wonderful! But it wasn't until 1994—when I was introduced to the Akashic Records—that I was satisfied. When I came upon the Records, I was unsure what they were or why I was so drawn to them. But when I opened them, I encountered an experience surprisingly similar to the one I had when I was 24: I felt known and loved, just the way I am. At that moment, I knew this was what I had been seeking!

After my introduction to the Records in 1994, my practice of doing readings for others began, followed by teaching others how to read their Records in 1996. By 2001, I was blessed with a download of the Pathway Prayer Process to Access the Heart of the Records. This happened in response to my plea to the Universe. I had asked for a simple resource that anyone who desired a conscious connection with their Soul could access. This distinction was important because prior access to the **Akasha** had been rooted in a belief that only a select few were entitled to connect with their Records.

In 2009, my first book, *How to Read the Akashic Records*, was released. It was the first book ever to share this process and these protocols. In it, you will find an instruction manual examining the organization and composition of the Records, as well as their application to our daily lives. With this, a movement was launched! In 2011, I followed it with *Healing Through the Akashic Records*, exploring healing for personal growth and transformation in the Akasha. The next pressing issue for me and many of my students was being spiritually awake and still participating effectively in the world. This quandary led to my writing *Discover Your Soul's Path Through the Akashic Records* in 2015. That same year, I was awarded a Doctorate of Spiritual Studies in the Akashic Records by the Emerson Theological Institute. I am proud to report that I am the first to earn this degree, which I personally designed! Most recently, in 2020, my pandemic baby was released: *Inspired Manifesting: Elevate Your Energy and Ignite Your Dreams Through the Akashic Records.*

As I hope you can tell, this has been quite a captivating path for me—one I never consciously planned, yet that continues to emerge as a central theme in my life. With every stage of personal growth, I have had the good fortune to be led, partnered, and followed by Akashic Light. It has offered more insight, guidance, and wisdom than I ever expected and given me a lifetime brimming with fulfillment.

PAUSE FOR SELF-REFLECTION

For a few minutes, think about your journey and consider what drew you to the Records. Questions inspire us and lead the way on our quests. What are yours? Pay attention; they are precious. Make note of them in a journal specially designated for this work.

LEVEL I

HOW TO READ THE AKASHIC RECORDS

L et's begin at the very beginning, with a meditation to become aware of Akashic Light. While you'll soon be prepared to do many exercises in your **Akashic Records**, you may not yet know how to access the Records. So for now, please read along. *You can also access a video of me guiding this meditation here: www.lindahowe.com /Akashic-Meditations.*

AKASHIC LIGHT MEDITATION I

As you gather your awareness for the journey at hand, seat yourself squarely, with your back straight but comfortable and supported, and your bottom connected to your seat, the floor, and the Earth. Exhale fully, expelling anything within you that interferes with your ability to be present. Now, inhale the present moment, allowing it to circulate within and through you, again, exhaling any distractions.

As you sit in your place, notice that there is a space on Earth that you alone occupy; you share it with no one else. You are the only individual in this unique location. Consider that Earth—even Life itself—has reserved this place for you. There is no substitute for you! Only once in all the ages do you exist, and here you are now! Let's awaken to this idea and allow ourselves to "take our place."

Now, get a sense of where you are and where your body is located. Rub your hands together and begin to draw energy up from the heart of the Earth. Draw it up from the very center of the planet through the root of your body. Allow it to travel into your body, through your legs, your trunk, your neck, and into the cavity of your skull. Allow this energy to press into the lining of your skull. By now, your hands should be warm. Use them to clear your aura, the energy field around your body. Physically brush off the space around you, clearing away any vibration on you or around you that is not yours and sending it into the Earth, where it can be absorbed and transmuted. When you are finished, place your hands in your lap, palms up.

Now allow yourself to become aware of Akashic Light—which is infinitely powerful, always present, and loving—hovering about 18 inches above your head. Your awareness of this Light strengthens it, causing activation, and it rains down over you—in front, behind, and on both sides. The Light clears away anything interfering with your ability to experience your goodness.

As the Light rains down from head to toe, it arrives under your feet and begins to gather, establishing a platform of Light holding you up, almost like a chair. Then the Light begins to fill your energy field. This egg-shaped space extends around you, about 18 inches in every direction—in front, behind, and on both sides. The Light fills that space, up to your ankles, knees, and hips, all the way to your shoulders and the top of your head. You are now sitting inside a Pillar of Light.

Let's take this moment to let the Light do its work. By its natural magnetic property, the Light draws from you anything that does not support you. This includes any physical pain, discomfort, or distress present; any emotional turbulence, worry, or chaos; and any thoughts that might be disturbing or upsetting you. The Light draws from you anything preventing your experience of ever-present inner peace. You do not have to tell the Light what to do; the Light is infinite intelligence that knows what you need at this moment. Just let it do its work.

And while the Light is drawing obstructions away from you by its magnetic nature, at the same time, by its radiant nature, it shines into you. This Light radiates into you from every angle possible—in front, above, behind, and below. As it passes through the boundary of your skin, it becomes what you need. So, if you need courage, the Light will become that. Perhaps you need comfort; the Light becomes that. Observe the Light as it becomes what you need. Let's take a few moments here to allow this to happen.

By now, you are in a state of good balance. In your mind's eye, open up the top of your head and let the Light pour into you through your crown, filling you up, meeting your every need. And, when you are full of Light, with no more space inside you, open your heart center from the inside, letting the Light flow from you in a stream down into the Earth. Consider that you are right here now. Open to the flow of Infinite Light into you through your crown, filling you up inside and pouring out through your heart center into the Earth. Now, expand your awareness to include everyone who has ever done this practice, forming a stream of Light down into the heart of the planet. Here, anchor the Light into the core of the Earth in any way that makes sense to you. Now, bring this Pillar of Light through the Earth, the room, the ceiling, the roof, to the edge of the consciousness of all our Akashic Lightworkers.

And from this location, we let it go where it will. Bring your attention back to your room. Expand the Light to press into the walls, the ceiling, and the floor. Now, expand the Light to connect with all around the world who are doing this work, setting up a spectacular field of Light covering the Earth so that we are all sitting within this space of Infinite Light perfectly calibrated for our consciousness.

And from this place, we begin our work. *And so we do acknowledge the Forces of Light, asking for guidance, direction, and courage to know the Truth as it is revealed for our highest good and the highest good of everyone connected to us.* Open your eyes now. If you'd like and it is safe to do so, light a candle as you do this work to serve as a reminder that we are here to enrich our relationship with this Light within and to shine Light into the world. When I teach, I keep an Akashic Candle lit as a symbol of the presence of Akashic Light. (NOTE: For your safety, please do not leave a lit candle unattended.)

LESSON ONE

ALL ABOUT THE
AKASHIC RECORDS

We begin our Akashic Adventure by learning all about the Akashic Records. How we understand the Records determines our relationship with them and how we use them. So, what is the Akashic Record? The Akashic Record is an infinite spiritual resource available for our support, growth, and transformation. "Akasha" is a Sanskrit word that means "primary substance—that from which all things are formed." It is the raw material of Life. We are dealing with the very essence of Life itself (before human entanglement with thoughts and feelings).

The Akashic Record is a vibrational archive of every Soul and its journey as human. Because it is vibrational, the Record is invisible. We never see the Record with our human eyes; you will never see a book, catalog, or library. And do not expect to see any images. We sense information in this realm primarily through our emotions. Next, we know it as an archive, collection, or treasury. The Record is composed of every person who has ever existed! Everyone is in it—no exceptions. All the people you know and love are included, as are all the people you do not like very much!

We can never erase anyone from the Record, nor can we ever be eliminated.

There are two parts to each set of Records: the first is fixed, and the second is evolving. The fixed part is permanent; think of it as Divine Potential or the DNA of the Soul. It is established at the Soul's inception and endures to the end of time. This essential, ultimate impression signifies your highest Truth. While the origin of Soul is a fascinating consideration—about which there are many opinions, each revealing an element of Truth—it is not helpful or necessary for work in the Akasha. Your way of interpreting the origin of Soul is welcome here. Soul is infinite, eternal, and mysterious.

The second part of each set of Records is growing, emerging, and constantly revealing itself to us as we transform. Think of this as the "Chronicles of You," a catalog or collection of stories of lifetimes you have lived through, awakening to your ultimate potential and living your highest expression while still in human form.

It may help to understand the Soul's journey from an Akashic point of view by considering an Akashic interpretation of the ancient idea of reincarnation. From an Akashic perspective, we are essentially perfect, whole, and complete at the core of our being. This is quite obvious when we do not have frail bodies. Still, when we're here on Earth incarnated as humans, we have a challenge to recognize our immense spiritual potential and an opportunity to live as our ideal, most loving self. We become aware of our Divine Potential through reincarnation and realize our Soul's perfection throughout lifetimes. As humans, our challenge is to love ourselves and others unconditionally, just as the Divine loves us. Reincarnation is the avenue through which we realize and live this Truth.

The Records are the intersecting zone of Heaven and Earth. It can be helpful to know that this is not exclusively the celestial realm nor the earthly dimension, but rather the zone where the two intersect and harmonize through us as humans. Many want to know where to find the Records. Where are they located? The answer is: everywhere! Accessible by a subtle shift in perception, they are within our reach.

Because this realm is infused in the fabric of our Soul, the Records are a Soul-level resource. The Records can be recognized as:

- The convergence zone of the Universal Mind, Heart, *and* Will (not just one, but all three);

- The energetic connective tissue from Soul to Source—emanating from Soul, keeping us connected to Source (but not *the* Source); and

- In practice, a bridge of Light for personal awakening and transformation.

Historically Speaking

As you may know, the Record is not new. Rather, it is an ancient spiritual resource accessible to modern spiritual seekers. The availability and understanding of the Akashic Records have evolved throughout history. Looking into the past, we can see the relationship between the Akashic Record and traditional religions. In fact, the Akasha is referred to in all major religions, the Judeo-Christian Bible being the one I am most familiar with. In Psalm 139, "The book of Life, the book of God's remembrance" is acknowledged. In ages past, there was some recognition of the Akashic Records. Even Ancient Greek philosophers Plato and Aristotle identified "The Field" as a comprehensive field holding all of Life and simultaneously woven through all of Life.

Continuing, we see references to the Records made by the Russian Theosophists in the 19th century, particularly Helena Blavatsky, who identified the Records. However, she could not describe how to make conscious contact with this resource. In the 20th century, German philosopher Rudolph Steiner coined the term "Akashic" when referring to a realm of light. In the 1940s and 50s, Edgar Cayce, the so-called "Sleeping Prophet" here in the United States, brought our collective attention to the Records. He was certainly brilliant in introducing the Akasha to the West, but because he was unconscious while engaging, he was unable to teach anyone "how to."

In the 1990s, there was a dramatic shift in the Record itself. For the first time in human history, secular people consciously accessed the **Akashic Realm**; it was no longer the exclusive domain of mystics, saints, and scholars. Ordinary people like you and me began to make this connection. While this has been a fascinating development for seekers around the world, many 21st century folks seek scientific validation about the existence of the **Akashic Field**. In 2004, Dr. Ervin László, an internationally renowned quantum physicist, shared his brilliant work on the matter in his breakthrough book *Science and the Akashic Field: An Integral Theory of Everything*. This work serves as the first scientific evidence of the existence of the Akashic Field. With great pride, I tell you that Dr. László has endorsed my work, including my first and fourth books, and his Club of Budapest has used the Pathway Prayer Process to Access the Records just as you are learning to do!

The Akashic Atmosphere

At this point, it is beneficial to make some distinctions that will help you have appropriate expectations of this work and your experience of the **Akashic Atmosphere**. This space is a spiritual one, as opposed to a psychic dimension. As a spiritual resource, it is rooted in love and open to any outcome, whereas the psychic realm is fear-based, intent on a preferred outcome and controlling circumstances until that preferred result is realized. While the Record is spiritual, no deity is involved, so there is no reason to offer sacrifices, petition, or pray to the Records. It is not *the Source*; rather, it is energy connecting us to the Source.

The **Akashic Records** are governed by Three Absolutes safeguarding the environment, and they are: *Fear Not*, *Judge Not*, and *Resist Not*. These Akashic Absolutes establish a spiritual sanctuary of reverence, kindness, respect, and compassion. Ultimately the Record is a safe space for examining and exploring profound Truths. "All Truth lies within," and yet we humans need safe spaces to allow the treasures of Truth embedded in our Souls to emerge. That safe, spiritual space is the Akasha.

Immersion in the Akashic Atmosphere is based on a primary assumption that everyone, without exception, is essentially good at the core.

From this, several logical ideas follow. Since everyone is good, we can expect their choices and actions to be good. The fundamental intention of every choice and action is a sincere desire to establish and expand a personal experience of being safe and loved. Although this may involve terrible behavior, the person initiating the behavior always executes it to expand their sense of being loved. Of course, everyone is always doing their best; no human ever decides to do less than their best in any given situation. If someone performs at a less than optimal level, you can be sure that it is the very best they can muster in that particular moment. We should include ourselves in this concept as well. There are times when we think we could be or do better, but we are more likely not as perfect as we hoped.

The Pathway Prayer Process

Now we turn our attention to the method we will be using to access the Akasha: The Pathway Prayer Process to Access the Heart of the Akashic Records. Let's take a look at the essential components and composition of the Prayer.

Consider the structure of the Prayer, which has two parts: the Opening Prayer and the Closing Prayer. To be successful, use both. The Opening Prayer has three Stanzas, each serving its own purpose. Stanza I is the Invocation, which begins, "And so." "To invoke" means to call in, which we are doing. It is always a good idea to know who you are praying to and what you are praying for. Here, we ask for assistance from the Forces of Light, requesting "guidance, direction, and courage to know the Truth." We are not asking for supernatural powers, to change other people, or to manipulate life circumstances. Why are we doing this? "For our highest good and the highest good of everyone connected to us."

In Stanza II, we consciously align with the Divine. While we are always aligned, we are not always aware of our connection with the Divine, and so our intention here is to awaken our awareness to the always-present connection we have with the Divine. This is not an old, white man. Instead, we address the spiritual presence that permeates every religious and spiritual belief.

the
Pathway Prayer *to* Access
the Heart *of the* Akashic Records©

OPENING PRAYER

I

And so we do acknowledge the Forces of Light,
Asking for guidance, direction, and courage to know the Truth
As it is revealed for our highest good and the highest good of
    everyone connected to us.

II

Oh Holy Spirit of God,
Protect me from all forms of self-centeredness
And direct my attention to the work at hand.

III

Help me to know (myself/first name of individual being read) in
    the Light of the Akashic Records,
To see (myself/first name of individual being read) through the eyes
    of the Lords of the Records,
And enable me to share the wisdom and compassion that the
    Masters, Teachers, and Loved Ones of (me/first name of
    individual being read) have for (me/him/her/them).
The Records are now open.

CLOSING PRAYER

I would like to thank the Masters, Teachers, and Loved Ones for
    their love and compassion.
I would like to thank the Lords of the Akashic Records for their
    point of view.
And I would like to thank the Holy Spirit of Light for all
    knowledge and healing.

The Records are now closed. Amen.
The Records are now closed. Amen.
The Records are now closed. Amen.

Next, we ask to be free of self-centered fears, our greatest challenge. Self-centered fear is a corrupting force that makes us vulnerable to the ego. Our attention is required elsewhere. Unnecessary focus on the self interferes with the flow of **Akashic Energy** and encourages inappropriate, egoic behavior. Watch out for self-doubt, performance concerns, perfectionism, etc., which prevent fulfilling work in the Records.

"Direct my attention to the work at hand" turns our thoughts to how we can be helpful. It is a simple but powerful directive. Service—expressing the love within—is a posture of immense power. As we offer to assist others, we are flooded with Light for our empowerment and those we serve. Service demonstrates the trust and confidence we have in the goodness of Life.

Stanza III invites our intention, goal, or purpose. In the first line, we want "to know" (meaning to comprehend and understand) within the Light of the Akashic Records, which is characterized by qualities of wisdom, compassion, and insight. We want to be able "to see through the eyes of the Lords of the Akashic Records," to have their infinite perspective. And we seek "to share the wisdom and compassion that the Masters, Teachers, and Loved Ones have for us." Indeed, we do!

And then, we announce out loud: "The Records are now open." This action respects our consciousness and our human reality at the moment. Spiritual maturity invites us to know where we are and take responsibility for the location of our awareness. When it comes to saying the Closing Prayer, as we all know, it is simply good manners to say, "Thank you!"

The Organization of the Records

The Akashic Records are relational and dynamic. We bring our human selves into this sacred space and are met with a loving, spiritual presence empowering us to awaken to the magnificent Truths of our being. With that in mind, let's consider the organization of the Akashic Records. From looking at the Prayer, we see a division of labor. Let's learn who these Beings of Light are and understand their roles and responsibilities.

The Lords of the Akashic Records are Beings of Light who never incarnate; they have never been in human form. We do not see them or interact with them directly. Instead, their attention is on the Record itself and keeping it healthy. Working together as a group without attention to personal identity, the Lords focus solely on maintaining the integrity of the Akashic Records.

Next, we have the **Masters**, which are Beings of Light who never incarnate but have been with us since the inception of our Souls when we make this connection. Their job is to accompany us, guiding and supporting our journey through time as humans; they are responsible for our spiritual awakening. As with the Lords, the Masters function as a group orchestrating our unfolding, with no need for personal attention. The most significant difference is that the Lords of the Records focus their attention on the Records, and the Masters focus their attention on us.

Teachers are also Beings of Light, ones who are not alive right now but may have been in bodily form at some point in time. They are theme- or lesson-specific specialists who stay with us until we embody their particular teaching (such as self-respect or self-trust), and then they move onto another Soul. Cooperating with other Teachers, they do not reveal their personal identities (unlike spirit guides or angels). This is also the level of our shared world teachers, such as Jesus, Lao Tse, and Kwan Yin, each of whom is responsible for bringing understanding of a certain spiritual principle to the world. Teachers are here for our growth, transformation, and to support us along the way.

Finally, we have **Loved Ones**, actual people we have known in this lifetime who are now deceased. Committed to the expanding awareness of our Souls and the Truth of our essence, they assist from the other side with comfort, encouragement, and guidance. You may have a sense of their presence. (NOTE: The Record is *not* the best resource for communicating with the dead; if that is your desire, please work with a skilled medium.)

I want to share some more information so you can become more confident about this spiritual resource and begin to see its potential when you open the Records:

- Angels and guides exist *outside* the Records; although they can be wonderful, they are *not* part of the Akashic Records.

- Akashic Records transmit the energy of the Akashic Field without personification. This work is not like trans-channeling, where perceived entities are allowed to occupy the body of the Practitioner. To dissolve perceived entities, look within and identify your fears. Ask for freedom from all fear. In the Records, we only allow Light to flow through us; we remain fully awake, alert, and retain agency. We are always the boss of ourselves!

- There is a significant difference between the Records and Shamanic Journeying. In a Journey, a Shaman leaves their body to travel to the Source of wisdom. They return to their body to share what they have obtained. We do *not* leave the body when working in the Records. The eighth chakra is where the individual Soul distinguishes itself from the Universal Soul. In the Records, the Soul distinguishes itself but never separates. When we open our Records, energy flows down into the crown of our head, landing in our heart center. It bounces off the floor of the heart space like a reflective surface and radiates out horizontally through the heart, forming a vertical/horizontal intersection.

- When we open the Records, we experience energy first, information second. The good news is that we do not have to evaluate it immediately; we can simply describe what it seems like we are getting. Because energy moves on the formed word, energy moves as we describe what is happening.

- Many students wonder how the guidance is transmitted. Approximately 5 percent of people *hear* wisdom from the Records, 10 percent *see images*, and 85 percent have a *sense of knowing*. I belong to the majority; rarely do I see images or hear messages. The only way to find out how you will receive insights from the Akasha is by actually working in your own Records.

Guidelines for Reading the Records

I have developed clear **Guidelines for Reading Your Own Akashic Records** to address your relationship with the Records and guide your success. I have noticed that students who follow these Guidelines have significantly better readings in the Records. You can handle your everyday life the way you see fit—these Guidelines are only concerned with your relationship with the Records. If you decide not to follow these Guidelines, your work in the Records may be weak, or you may not have any ability to read your Records. With this in mind, let's consider each one:

1 Do not consume drugs or alcohol for 24 hours before opening the Records. These substances weaken the edge of your energy field and cause a loss of authority over your experience. We want to be clear and strong when doing spiritual work.

2 Every name has a vibration, a spiritual probability. When opening the Records, use your current legal name (listed on legal documents such as a government ID or mortgage). This may be your birth name or not. Naming calls forth the vibrational archive of your Soul.

3 Be responsible for your time in the Records. Decide before entering how long you plan to stay. Ten minutes is a good minimum, and there is never any reason to keep your Records open for longer than an hour. If you want to continue your exploration, all you need to do is close your Records, take a short break, and then reopen them later. It takes practice to build your "spiritual muscle" in the Records. Give yourself a chance to develop yours. Do not leave your Records open while you go to work or when you go to sleep. At work, you are being paid to bring the full use of your human faculties, not to be in a slightly altered state. When we sleep, we don't have authority over ourselves or the process—having your Records open while sleeping will not improve your dreams or enhance your work in the Records. Stick to one activity at a time!

4 Ground yourself after each reading by doing any activity
that reminds you that you are indeed a human being: drink
water, eat something, walk your dog, water your plants,
wash your dishes, etc. Keep it simple; just be sure to do it.

5 When combining the Akashic Records with any other system,
always honor the guidelines for both systems. After the first 30
days of practice, you may consider mixing this with another
complementary method once you know this energy and how
it affects you. Personally, I don't because I find the Records
more than adequate, but some people like to add this onto their
already-existing practice of Reiki, feng shui, and astrology.

Now, let's learn the steps involved in opening your own Akashic
Records, mastering this before attempting to do this work for others. But you need not wait to open the Records until you've read this
entire section or book. *Now* is the perfect time to begin.

HOW TO READ YOUR OWN AKASHIC RECORDS

This is a perfect time to open your own Records. Think of it as standing at the shore of a fabulous ocean. While you may want to run into the deepest part, you know it is best to give yourself a chance to get used to the water and ease into other conditions before heading in further. Begin by reading all three Stanzas of the Opening Prayer out loud. Then, return to the third Stanza and read it silently twice more, using your current legal name, for a total of three times. Next, announce out loud: "The Records are now open." Once your Records are open, describe what is happening to the best of your ability. You may see, hear, or sense something, nothing, or maybe a great deal of things are occurring. There is no reason to figure everything out. Simply describe your experience, especially your emotions. To close the Records, read the Closing Prayer out loud. Make some notes.

How to Experience Your Own Records

Open your Records. Begin by giving yourself a chance to get used to being in the Records. There is a quality described as the Akashic Atmosphere, governed by these Three Absolutes: *Fear Not, Judge*

Not, Resist Not. These Absolutes make sure the Realm is emotionally safe and supportive. Notice the felt sense of being in your Akashic Records. How does it feel? What emotions do you experience? Observe your level of comfort. Invite the presence of your loving Masters, Teachers, and Loved Ones (from here on called "**MTLOs**"). Even though you have never seen them, sense into a feeling that they are around you, completely understanding and loving you.

Now, ask your MTLOs to help you recognize yourself and your human story over time, from the perspective of Light, Truth, and Compassion. You may become aware of yourself becoming more awake and loving as your Soul goes from one lifetime to another. It becomes increasingly easier to be kind and generous with yourself and others. You are a remarkable being.

Next, go a bit deeper. Ask the MTLOs to assist you so you can get a sense of yourself in this lifetime, within the context of your Soul's entire journey as human. What is significant about this lifetime? What is important about who you are and the life you are living? What are the most significant opportunities being presented to you in this life? This is a good time to ask for help in recognizing the value of your human experience at this time in your Soul's evolution and the whole of human awakening. Close the Records and make some notes.

Now that we've learned the basics, let's put this knowledge into practice with the following Empowerment Exercise in your Records. If this is your very first time opening your own Records, open your mind and heart to this new experience. Focus on the questions raised and the answers received, even if they seem vague. It is helpful to journal while in your Records. Simply write whatever comes into your awareness. Do not evaluate; just make notes on your insights. Making notes validates your work, which adds energy to your growth process and, over time, helps you go deeper into the Records. Describe what it "seems like" you are getting. This is how to activate the flow of Akashic Energy. Keep in mind that there are no "right" or "wrong" answers to these questions, which are designed to support your explorations in the Akasha. It's important that you give yourself enough time to experiment in the Records. I recommend at least 30 minutes.

EMPOWERMENT EXERCISE #1
How to Read the Akashic Records

To consider your current relationship with the Akasha, open your Akashic Records using the Opening Prayer and explore the following questions:

- Why am I prompted to work in the Records at this specific point in my life?

- Why this particular Prayer?

- What are the purposes of this work for me at this time in my life?

- Ask to see your life story (in this lifetime) the way it is seen and known in the Akashic Records. Look for spiritual themes and motivators and how they intersect with the ordinary elements of your life.

- Inquire: How can I be more open and receptive to the Akashic Records and my MTLOs for guidance and direction in my life?

Close the Records using the Closing Prayer. Make some notes.

PAUSE FOR SELF-REFLECTION

Self-awareness is the key to becoming an effective Practitioner. Share your discoveries with a trustworthy friend. Please DO NOT read another person's Records until you are comfortable reading your own Records. For now, just focus on yourself. Each time you open the Records, please consider the following questions:

- Do you think you are in your Records?

- What happened that leads you to believe so?

- Do you think you did not connect with your Records?

- Why not? What convinced you that you were not?

- In either case, what clues or hints support your decision?

• Describe/evaluate your connection with your
own Records. For example, how are you receiving
information? Do you see, hear, or sense it?

• What is most comfortable? What is most confusing?

• Are you able to describe what is happening or not?

• Are you able to restrain yourself from trying to "figure it
all out" before you have completed your exploration?

Strengthening Your Connection with the Akashic Records

One of the most common questions students ask is how to strengthen
their connection with the Records. The following practice addresses
this very issue. We accommodate more spiritual light by being fully
grounded as ordinary human beings. I like to think of this as our
"Spiritual Fitness Exercise," keeping us in fit spiritual condition on a
daily basis. The purpose of this practice is to strengthen your relationship with your Records, empowering your deeper connection with
Akashic Light and Wisdom. With regular use, you can effectively clear
away obstructions and resolve human blockages to your connection
with your Records. This particular exercise is the absolute best preparation for being an optimal agent for Akashic Light. While this may
be your first time exploring this particular exercise, note that we will
revisit Spiritual Fitness at each Level.

EMPOWERMENT EXERCISE #2
Spiritual Fitness

Open your Records using the Pathway Prayer Process. Settle in and get
comfortable. Scan the space around your body. Describe the Akashic
Atmosphere, identifying the specific qualities you encounter. For example, you may have a sense of peace, safety, security, or other loving

qualities. Direct your attention within. Survey your general well-being. How are you today? Describe your overall sense of how you are doing.

Think about your physical self. Note your strengths and weaknesses at the moment. For example, you may feel very robust but have some aches and pains. Describe your physical well-being to yourself, identifying the particulars, both positive and negative. Ask your MTLOs to assist you with your physical well-being today. Whether you need more energy or pain relief, the Universe has a solution for every difficulty you encounter. You can ask for guidance to relieve any physical issues you have, as well as wisdom for building your physical power.

Bring your attention to your emotional state today. How are you feeling? Are you happy, sad, angry, worried, or some combination of emotions? Notice your feelings and identify them. Excitement, happiness, sadness, and worry are all acceptable emotions. Ask your MTLOs to give you the emotional support you need today. Whether that is confidence, comfort, or compassion, the Universe is ready to meet your emotional needs. You can always ask for suggestions to relieve any unpleasant or difficult feelings and invite recommendations for cultivating a more serene, happier state of being.

Now, notice any activity in your mind. What kind of thoughts are you thinking today? Are you entertaining ideas that give you peace of mind or thoughts that make you fearful? This is an area of great power for people! We can select our own thoughts. Notice your pattern of thinking and decide whether it brings you greater peace or more distress. You are the chooser! You get to choose what you think! Make an inspired choice, requesting the assistance of your MTLOs. Ask them to empower you to direct your thinking so you can have more positive outcomes today.

Now, look to this day—just this day. Review the activities you are likely to experience, the people you expect to spend time with, your goals and intentions for the day ahead. There may be some enjoyable activities and others that you are not so happy about. In your Records, ask for assistance meeting the unfolding day with confidence and compassion. You can request that guidance and wisdom meet you at every juncture of the day, knowing they will be there when you arrive. If you are facing a particular issue, this is a good time to ask for insight, guidance, or wisdom to support you as you deal with it. Ask for a special message for today and hold it in your heart. This message may be a word, phrase, or even a sentiment—something you can place in your heart that takes root and grows as a part of your consciousness.

Close your Records.

PAUSE FOR SELF-REFLECTION

Now is a good time to reflect on your work in the Records so far. You may have dramatic experiences, or you may wonder if you are even finding the Records. This is a learning process, so give yourself a chance to learn! The following questions can help guide you toward your fulfillment. You may want to journal about these. Do not open your Records for this exploration. Just use your ordinary faculties to support your spiritual journey. Whether you feel you are connecting with your Records or not, ask yourself the following questions:

- What leads me to believe that I was in my Akashic Records?

- What happened or didn't happen to suggest I was in the Records?

- What makes me think I was not in my Akashic Records?

- What led me to believe I was not in my Records?

Tips for Success

There are a few areas to clarify to help you on your quest. It is beneficial to understand the relationship between the Records and intuition, imagination, the subconscious, and the higher mind. Overall, be realistic!

Talent + Skill + Practice = Success

While you may or may not have a natural talent for this work, I intend to give you the tools you need to refine your gift and deliver the highest quality spiritual services to yourself and others, if you choose. In your self-evaluation, describe what the experience "seems like" rather than trying to figure out what anything means. This will accelerate the flow of Akashic Energy and wisdom. Most work in the Records requires more than one visit. Take your time to examine the issues, explore possible solutions, and describe whatever you are getting or not. This is how to make space for the Truth to reveal itself. Also, framing effective questions for productive results in the Records can distinguish between satisfaction and frustration in your practice. Powerful questions are rooted in a solid understanding of the Records and appropriate expectations for this spiritual resource.

Remember, when working in the Records, we are exploring, not divining, the future. There is a big difference between the two. Exploration requires trust—in Life and ourselves—and open-mindedness about outcomes. Divination (or fortune-telling) seeks a preferred answer based on fear. We often seek to know or control the future when we are afraid. Many "Yes/No" questions fall into this category. The Records are of little help with this type of question. If this is what you want, it may be best to get a pendulum or other psychic instrument.

Equally, issues of time are especially challenging in the Records. When we enter the Akashic Realm, ordinary time as we know it here on Earth collapses. In the Records, the past, present, and future are available and accessible now. "Now" is the most authentic measure of time in the Records. All of time is present but only available to us as it addresses our current concerns. When we ask a "when" question, we bring forth a response having more to do with the sequence of events than a date on a calendar. Time, as we know it on Earth, does not matter in the Records. What is vital in our Records is expanding and developing our spiritual awareness. Asking "When will I meet my soulmate?" is typically met with a response like this: "After you make peace with your ex, resolve your relationship with your sister, and clean the mess in your garage, you'll be ready to meet your mate." The Records do not have any opinion about when we take those actions; it is up to us whether to do them quickly or slowly. Either way, these actions help us become who we are meant to be and grow into our potential—the sacred Truth held in our Records.

Because our spiritual development is woven into our human journey, questions about human challenges illuminate spiritual concerns. We can start with ordinary human concerns such as relationships, health, and work, and spiritual underpinnings will emerge. Spiritual themes are revealed through our human experiences, so begin with everyday human issues, and you will more easily arrive at a powerful understanding of your Soul's Purposes. When in the Records, describe your challenges, including the mundane aspects of any issue. Energy moves on the formed word, and as we "describe," energy moves.

Intuition, Imagination & the Higher Self

To clarify the relationship between intuition and the Akashic Records, it may help to conduct a simple experiment that will reveal a wealth of information. To do this experiment, bring a question you have about yourself to your intuition and the Records. This question needs to be something about your everyday life like relationships, work, creative projects, health, etc. Make notes on your findings. Scope and perspective are the most significant differences between intuition and the Records; both are valuable and important. Intuition is held within the Records but is more limited in range, only specific to you at this point. The Records are more comprehensive, including the context of your entire Soul's journey as human.

For a comparison, consider the relationship between house lights and a single spotlight in a theater. The house lights are comparable to the Akashic Records and the spotlight represents your intuition in this metaphor. When the house lights are on, you can see the entire complex, including all spaces within the theater. Think of the spotlight as your intuition; it is extremely valuable for seeing a particular space. When the house lights are turned off and the spotlight is shining, you can see a specific area clearly, but not the context.

Your imagination is a great place to begin your spiritual explorations, even in the Records. It is the gift to launch you into higher realms of spiritual insight, guidance, and wisdom. And yet it can be confusing to students. Imagination is a wonderful spiritual tool gifted to every human being. The wonders of your imagination are within you and part of the Universal imagination. Having taught thousands of individuals to work in the Records, I am continually amazed when students worry that they are merely imagining guidance even when the insights they receive are so perfectly designed for them. Because intuition is held within the Records, and the higher self is an agent or instrument of the intuition, it is also a slice of the Records.

Another area people often inquire about is the relationship between the subconscious and the Records. Recall that the Akashic Field is composed of the convergence of the Universal Heart, Mind, and Will. Your subconscious is one section of your Mind, which is one-third of the Akashic Field. So, the subconscious is a part of the Record, but not the entire Record.

With this useful information, you are now prepared to work in the Records of others. Come with me to the next Lesson, where we will learn how to do effective readings for others.

HOW TO READ THE RECORDS OF OTHERS

have noticed that students are attracted to this work due to an inner prompting, an urge from their Souls, and that they naturally have the raw talent and ability to succeed. They come to me seeking basic training to empower them to use their natural gifts. As I understand it, students bring the talent, and as their teacher, I provide the skill-building so they can serve others in deep and meaningful ways. It is that simple and that wonderful. Working with others is one of the fastest ways to learn. So, even if you think you may never do a reading for another person, please keep an open mind and participate in this part of the process so you can be as successful as possible.

Guidelines & Recommendations

When reading the Akashic Records of others, we use the Guidelines for Success mentioned above, with some expansion because we are working with the MTLOs of others. Following the Guidelines can make all the difference between your effectiveness and ineffectiveness. As in all things, the Golden Rule applies: Do unto others as you would have them do unto you. Do your best but please do not worry about making mistakes—we all make mistakes! If you make an error while working in the Records and are sincerely sorry for the mistake, you will be fine. There is a special grace to cover our learning errors. So, do not be afraid to try—the Akashic Light is ready to catch you when you slip!

1 No alcohol or drugs for the **Practitioner** for at least 24 hours before doing a reading.

2 Only do readings in real time and ideally in person, although readings by phone call, Zoom, Skype, or other real-time communication methods are acceptable. While you can use email and other forms of written communication to convey information about readings (such as availability, timing, and process), you may *not* do readings by email (where a client sends you questions and you respond).

3 Make no recommendations for the client. You are reading the Soul, not the energy field.

4 Their legal name is required: use the name the client uses on legal documents right now, not their birth name. You will also want to know their name and pronouns so you can address them appropriately, but always use their legal name when saying the Prayer silently.

5 The Practitioner is the timekeeper of the reading. As the Practitioner, you are in charge of time! Let your client know in advance how long the reading will be. Thirty minutes is a reasonable amount of time for a reading, especially when you are new to the Records. Never spend more than an hour in the Records. It is better to do 30 powerful, helpful minutes with a client than to waste their time and yours with 60 minutes. If the client has more questions and wants you to keep going, be disciplined and schedule a follow-up session.

6 Be sure to ground yourself before and after the reading. Get some fresh air or something to eat. It helps to reconnect to the ordinary day.

7 Before opening anyone's Records, obtain their permission. *DO NOT READ ANYONE'S RECORDS WITHOUT THEIR EXPRESS PERMISSION.* This means that we do not read the Records of the deceased, those in a coma, or anyone unable to ask. If they cannot make the request, they are not meant to have a reading. The request must be in ordinary life, not through a dream or encounter with someone's higher self. You can, of course, offer the requester a reading. For example, if a friend or relative asks you to open the Records of someone in dire straits, you need to say, "No," but you can certainly offer them a reading. You may say something like, "I am sorry I cannot open the Records of _____, but I would be happy to open yours if you like."

8 Maintain the strictest confidentiality. Readings are private; do not share what you find with anyone other than the client. Do not post on social media about a session you did or the great healing you facilitated in another. Keep quiet. If your client wants to share their session, it is their decision. As a Practitioner, it is not your place to share.

9 Present all information as positively as possible. Simply describe what it "seems like" is happening, steering away from judgment and evaluation. Keep the client's question in mind. Let the client determine the meaning.

10 Every reading aims to dignify and elevate the person being read—to reveal that person's true self and potential. Gently and respectfully share everything that a person's MTLOs reveal, even if it makes you uncomfortable, seems insignificant, or doesn't make sense to you. Sometimes, the things that you hold back from saying are what a person most needs to hear. Be sure to describe what you are receiving rather than evaluate it; give your client the chance to reflect and interpret the meaning and value of the reading.

11 *DO NOT OPEN THE RECORDS OF CHILDREN/ANYONE UNDER THE AGE OF 18.* Children need to develop as human beings first and foremost. Each culture has its own

definition of when a child becomes an adult. The Pathway Prayer Process honors the cultural norms of the US, the place of origin of this system. The United States generally recognizes adulthood as 18 years of age. Until children reach the age of 18, they are the legal responsibility of their parents or guardians and cannot make their own legally binding choices. Since having an Akashic Record reading requires individuals to take responsibility for their own actions, children must wait until they are 18 to have a reading. If someone insists that they are mature and ready to access the Records at 17 (or younger), tell them you will be around when they are 18. That said, parents can open their own Records and ask questions about raising their children.

Recommendations for the First 30 Days of Practice

- *Invite* others to have a reading. There is a big difference between inviting and insisting. If they say yes, go for it and have fun. If they say no, you must respect their answer. When inviting someone, try something like this: "I just learned how to do these readings; can I try it out on you?" This way, they are not worried about your Akashic Records knowledge. If they know you are brand new, they will not expect a miracle! This will enable you to learn without pressure to perform.

- When you begin, do not collect money for your Akashic readings. After the first 30 days of consistent readings for others, you can charge whatever you like. I suggest asking in your Records for recommendations and using good common sense. Pay attention and be flexible. You will be led to the optimal payment amount for your services.

- If you are interested in combining the Records with another complementary method, please practice for at least 30 days before mixing methods. Make sure you know the energy of the Records and how you respond to them. Then, be absolutely certain that you honor the guidelines of both systems.

How to Open the Records of Another Person

- Obtain the current legal name of the client and use their name and personal pronouns.

- Read the first Stanza of the Prayer out loud.

- Read the first line of the second Stanza out loud, followed by silently reading the next two lines.

- Read the third Stanza out loud one time, using the first name of your client.

- Next, read the third Stanza silently two times, using the current legal name of your client.

- Announce the opening of the Records by saying, "The Records are now open."

- Do not memorize the Prayer. It is more powerful when read as directed.

Remember that this is not a psychic reading, so you are not expected to know your client's deep secrets or the future. Your job is to examine, explore, and assist your client in recognizing the spiritual/loving opportunities of their situation. Keep your eyes open and ask your client questions about their challenge. Present all the information you get as positively and respectfully as possible. Please be kind. When first learning how to do readings for others, many of us find ourselves in an awkward position. We do not know what we are doing. Relax! You are free to explore and even to make mistakes. As long as you are sincere in your desire to be helpful, it will all work out.

Working in the Records of Nonhumans (Pets, Plants, Crystals & Places)

Working in the Records of nonhumans can be a lot of fun—although success is not guaranteed for everyone. When doing Akashic Records readings, our primary focus is on people and improving the quality of their life experiences. Other areas of concern are secondary, and only a few will succeed. So, before we go any further, lower your expectations and open your mind. Be open to where you fall on the continuum! If this is your work, you will succeed; otherwise, probably not.

When we talk about "Examining Planetary Life through the Akashic Lens," we are speaking about opening the Akashic Records of pets, plants, places—and even planets! Because the Akashic Record is the archive of all Souls as humans on Earth, we want to keep in mind that every step we take away from humans and toward animals, plants, and other beings is a step away from clarity and density and a move toward the vague and abstract. This is not a problem; it is simply the reality of this dimension. Although the same Guidelines and Protocols apply when opening the Records of another person, let's take a closer look at how to do this and what we can expect.

With pets, use the current name of the pet. Of course, you need the pet owner's permission; you cannot just wander around and open the Records of stray animals. Ask the animal if they want a reading. They will not sit for readings but will give a nod of recognition or a sneer. Respond accordingly! When working in the Records of an animal, you have the opportunity to glimpse the reasons they are having trouble. While the Records are wonderful for diagnosis and background for issues animals face, you will not be having a long discussion with the Soul of an animal. The Records are not a good resource for that. However, if you seek clarity and guidance about health or behavior issues an animal is exhibiting, the Records can be extremely helpful.

Plants are fascinating. It is best to open the Records of the plant group with the species name since an individual flower or plant is too weak to be read clearly. So, you can open the Records of the species (like azaleas or ferns) and ask about the healing properties and Soul-level intentions of that particular plant group. The Records are excellent for searching out the healing potentials of a plant group and learning how to use them. Note that you will *not* be having an in-depth discussion with the plant.

Crystals are fascinating! Open by the group name (quartz, amethyst, etc.) and ask for insight into the purposes of the crystal. If you have an individual crystal with a powerful connection and a name, you can try to open the Records and ask about the intentions of that particular crystal. Depending on the crystal and your relationship, anything can be revealed.

Places are fun and so informative. You are always welcome to open the Records of any place on the planet, including oceans, rivers, mountain ranges, deserts, and the like. If you want to open the Records of a city or a country, you can. Naturally, you will only receive what is there for you to receive. If you have a strong connection to a place, you may get much better results from opening your own Records and asking about that location. This can be helpful, especially if you want to move to another part of the world. It is worth a try to see what you can discover.

If you are curious about a place such as a home or an office space, you can open the Records of that place only if your name is on the title or lease. If it is for sale on an open listing, you can open the Records; but if it is not for sale, do not go there—that is unethical. The Records of a dwelling can reveal the higher purpose of the place. Some years back, I had a great experience when a woman came to me asking about a house she wanted to purchase. She was worried because the previous owners had all moved after three or four years; she was afraid it was haunted or something. The house was for sale on multiple listings, so we opened the Records using the address. I asked about the intentions of this place and became aware that the house dedicated itself to empowering its residents. Everyone who lived there was encouraged and inspired to reach for more in their career—and they did just that! So, my client went to the neighbors and learned that the prior owners had all received promotions, and that's why they had moved on after just a few years. Knowing this information, she and her husband bought the house—and a few years later, he got a promotion, and they moved to the West Coast. It was perfect.

What do you think? Are you ready to give this a try and open the Records of a pet, plant, crystal, or place? Now is your opportunity. Remember, it's not for everyone. Feel free to move on if this doesn't feel enlivening to you.

EMPOWERMENT EXERCISE #3

Opening the Records of a Nonhuman

Pick one (pet, plant, crystal, or place) and open the Records. Simply describe what it seems like. Close the Records. Make some notes.

PAUSE FOR SELF-REFLECTION

Now is a good time to assess whether you are connecting with your Records. As you've engaged in the Records, what have you noticed as "clues" or "evidence"? What seems to occur when you are in the Records that leads you to believe you are successful? On the other hand, what is happening to convince you that you are not in the Records? As your understanding and compassion for yourself and others grow, you can be sure you are in the Records—this is the most reliable benchmark for determining whether you have been successful. Psychic phenomena are fascinating but not an indication of whether you are in the Records. As a spiritual resource, the Akashic Record is made of love. And love in its countless expressions is the best evidence of whether we have made contact in the Records.

AKASHIC PERSPECTIVES ON HEALING & TRANSFORMATION

The purpose of an Akashic Records reading is to dignify the individual being read. In these readings, we can recognize the person and their current issues from their Soul's perspective. The perspective of the Soul is spiritual, which is unconditionally loving. We can grasp a person and their circumstances through this exquisite lens of unconditional love. Our work is in the family of spiritual counseling instead of psychic reading. Spiritual counseling is rooted in love and oneness, trusting in the goodness of Life, and is open to any outcome. Psychic readings are based on fear of people, places, situations, Life, and anything else. They compel people to seek information to avoid discomfort or to control or manipulate an outcome.

Self-Love

There is a critical distinction between self-love and self-indulgence. Love is based on humility rooted in accurate self-assessment: recognizing all of God is within me, but I am *not* all of God. Honoring that I am both an infinite, eternal, immortal Soul *and* a finite, temporal, mortal human. This is true for each of us individually and all of us together. Every human being is designed this way. While we are all unique expressions of the Divine, we are not special, nor are we the only ones with Divine Magnificence residing within. While our spiritual growth supports our unconditional regard for ourselves, it does not give us license to indulge selfishness or immaturity. True self-love involves discipline, responsibility, commitment, and honorable service.

Reincarnation

As we work in the Records, we increasingly find information suggesting the reality of reincarnation. Reincarnation is the idea that a Soul lives many lifetimes, assuming many different human identities throughout time. From the Akashic point of view, the purpose of reincarnation is to learn to appreciate and enjoy who we are, to allow ourselves to love and be loved, and to be of fulfilling service and usefulness to others even though we are imperfect humans. Reincarnation allows and embraces the experience of our spiritual magnificence while fully honoring our human selves. Throughout our countless lifetimes, we have unlimited opportunities to expand our ability to appreciate and understand ourselves and others until we achieve a state of unconditional love: the goal of the Soul's journey as human.

As humans, we are naturally imperfect, which can lead to us berating ourselves in an effort to overcome our human vulnerabilities. Unconditional self-love is our primary spiritual opportunity. In practical terms, this means we open our hearts to ourselves, especially when experiencing a difficult time with our imperfect behavior or thoughts. At times such as this, we say to ourselves: "It's okay. No wonder you did that; it looked like a good idea. Of course you have these feelings; you are a real person. It's all right." Use words that are comfortable to you to convey understanding and acceptance for yourself.

One significant benefit of spiritual awakening is that we consciously allow the Light of Life to use us, even though we are imperfect human beings. Our flaws and limitations do not prohibit the Light from shining through us for our own happiness and that of others. Even in human form, we can give and receive love. Perfection is not required! The value of our spiritual awareness is usefulness, not perfection. Life can, will, and does use us to be a blessing to ourselves and everyone else; we need not be perfect.

Wounds

All humans throughout time experience wounds or injuries. There are no exceptions; this is a shared planetary experience. Let's examine the Akashic point of view concerning wounds and shift from an ordinary to a sacred perspective. For ages, the idea was that our wounds were evidence of our unworthiness—proof that we were unenlightened sinners. Our new idea is that every wound is an opportunity to connect with the infinite essence within us and experience unconditional self-love: to learn to love ourselves no matter what.

Many of us would prefer to leave victim consciousness behind, but until we accept and appreciate the victim mindset, we are doomed to repeat it. To go beyond this painful state of being, we can apply the practice of unconditional self-love to victimization. Ask yourself, "How do I love myself even when I have been a victim? How do I love another even when they have a victim experience?" Our willingness to accept and love amid victimization transforms the root of the pattern, liberating the person involved and transcending the wound.

Accelerating our healing is paramount to most of us. My Records revealed this turbo-charged healing question to radically transform any problem. No matter what the difficulty, ask yourself: "How can I love myself while I have this undesirable situation? How do I love and appreciate myself when I am not meeting my standards?" When dealing with others, ask these questions: "Can I understand that they are doing their best, that every choice they made and action they took was an effort to expand their experience of being loved? Do I recognize that this person is completely lovable even though they are facing a tough situation? How do I love and respect them even though they are currently embroiled in this difficulty? How can we get a sense of the reality that, even though we are addressing human imperfections, infinite love within prevails?"

We are all brimming with Light and love, able to give and receive even while imperfect. Bask in the reality of that!

PAUSE FOR SELF-REFLECTION

Here, at the halfway point of Level I, let's take this opportunity to observe your progress. I have introduced you to the Records, including basic background information covering their nature, organization, and composition. I've presented Guidelines for successful practice and how to apply the process using the Pathway Prayer. You now have a clear idea about appropriate and inappropriate expectations for this work. You have identified some simple yet powerful approaches to understanding your human experience through an Akashic lens. You are gradually becoming more comfortable in the Records, finding ease of connection, access, and communication. Don't worry about progress; just keep focusing on the work at hand and turning your thoughts to the issues presented at the moment.

Next, we will open our Records to gain a deeper connection and clearer understanding of our Soul's journey as a human.

EMPOWERMENT EXERCISE #4
Your Soul's Journey as a Human

Open your Records using the Pathway Prayer protocol. Take a few moments to center into your Records. Make note of the qualities of the Akashic Atmosphere and describe what you find. Open your awareness to the loving presence of your MTLOs. Even though you never see them, you can always detect their presence. In their compassionate company, ask to get a sense of yourself as you are recognized in the Light of Truth or to see yourself as they identify you.

You may see images, hear suggestions, or have a felt sense of yourself. All are valid ways to receive guidance within your Records. It may be that you simply sense being in a safe, sacred space, where you are completely accepted as you are, and the core loving goodness inside of you is free to come out into the world.

Now, get more specific, looking for particular aspects of who you are. As you are held in this Akashic Light, what do you see as your most vital personal traits? Get a sense of the strengths and virtues you have cultivated over lifetimes. Focus on the loving traits you have been developing for countless centuries. Direct your attention to how you have been learning to listen to yourself, trust your inner wisdom, and express yourself in this life. Notice the treasure trove of wisdom and compassion you hold in your heart/mind. Here, on this very day, you find all the insight, understanding, and love you have been cultivating for ages. And all of it is right here within you, now.

Notice the profound commitment your Soul has to you living your magnificence, how your faith and trust in yourself, Life, and the Ultimate Reality have been strengthened in both good and challenging times. Sense the remarkable creativity you have and the persistent, continuous, deliberate attention the Divine has for you. Open up to this enduring, amazing partnership between your Soul and the Ultimate Reality. Know that there is absolutely nothing you can do to sever this connection. This eternal partnership endures no matter what you do or fail to do, as well as what any other person does or fails to do to you. It is possible to hide from this relationship, minimize it, or ignore it, but it is an energetic impossibility to disconnect from this sacred bond. Take a moment to allow yourself to grasp your unshakeable connection to the infinite, anchored in unconditional love for you—now, today, and always.

Close your Records. Pause and make some notes on your experience.

FUNDAMENTAL PRINCIPLES FOR HEALING IN THE RECORDS

To hasten your growth, let's review a few of the principles for healing in the Records. Remember that the purpose of an Akashic Records reading is to dignify the individual being read. As Practitioners, we have the chance to perceive the person and their challenges from the point of view of their Soul. This is the perspective of unconditional love. So, when we work in the Records, we glimpse who a person is and the issues they face through the lens of unconditional love. In practice, this means that we search and find the valid, sound reasons they made their life choices. We then shine the Light on their efforts to expand their experience of love in everyday life. Sometimes this is very easy, and at other times, it can be more difficult. Either way, this form of spiritual counseling can transform a person's experience.

Clearing Stuck Karma

A key concept for all spiritual seekers is Karma. Let's examine Karma through the Akashic lens to recognize it within ourselves, understand its purpose, and most importantly, learn how to clear it. First identified by the Buddha in approximately 500 BCE, Karma is the law of cause and effect. For every effect, there is a cause. For every manifestation, there is an initial idea, followed by an action bringing it into form. Every idea has a natural, external manifestation. The idea is within us, and the expression is outside of us. Every consequence or result has an originating notion. This is neither good nor bad; it simply is how Life works.

Sometimes, this pattern of cause and effect repeats itself, playing out until we accept the reality of the cause/effect relationship and begin to make different choices that bring about other effects or results. This process is natural. However, the process stalls when we have a negative opinion or judgment about the cause, the effect, or the people involved. Our condemnation brings the cycle to a halt until we make peace with the cause/effect or the people involved. Negative opinion, judgment, or condemnation cause the process to get jammed up or stuck. This is the nature of negativity. It is not personal; it works this way for everyone. The intensity of our negativity freezes the flow, and we are caught in the pattern until we find a solution. If negative judgment is the problem, then acceptance is the solution.

Once acceptance has been introduced into the cycle, the dynamic changes. Acceptance facilitates release. This does not imply approval but involves a basic recognition of the ideas underpinning and driving the demonstration. And it necessitates an acceptance or recognition, without judgment, of the process and the people involved. When we decide that either the cause or the consequence of anything is bad or wrong, our negative assessment keeps the pattern in place. But, as we relinquish negative judgments about any situation, resistance ceases, and we move toward acceptance. *Acceptance facilitates release!* As we make peace with who we are and who we have been in all circumstances, we gain freedom from our stuck Karma. The patterns of cause and effect collapse in an atmosphere of understanding and acceptance.

A situation that does not make logical sense and is seemingly unbudgeable is likely to be Karmic. This indicates you have a negative idea about how things are or "should" be. Karma is not between us and another; it is within us. Any outside participant is simply mirroring our beliefs for the purpose of our healing.

Here are the fundamentals for clearing stuck Karma:

- Accept the person, the situation, and yourself "as is." Relinquish judgment.

- Recognize the undesirable pattern. Identify the ideas and actions (causes) stimulating the response or effect.

- Acknowledge and accept the human reality of the situation.

- A grievance is a complaint indicating a negative assessment or judgment.

- The number one block to experiencing good is grievances against the self.

- Recognize every pattern as positive at the point of origin (when we selected the idea/behavior). We only and always choose our best option to facilitate greater love and inner peace. *There are no exceptions to this rule!*

You are undoubtedly seeing that the best way to apply what you learn is through practice in the Records. So let's do another Empowerment Exercise in your Records. Given the nature of Karma and the power of this exercise to accelerate your transformation, you may find yourself using this one frequently!

EMPOWERMENT EXERCISE #5
Clear Your Karma & Accelerate Your Transformation

Open your Records using the established protocol. Get settled in the loving company of your MTLOs. Feel their support even though you cannot see them. In their compassionate presence, bring to mind a complaint you have about yourself: a human trait, failing, shortcoming, etc.—something you do or do not do. Describe the behavior and the consequences of this behavior. Ask your MTLOs to shine Akashic Light on this matter.

Within this space of infinite respect and understanding, ask yourself:

- When did this start? What happened? (Stay within this lifetime.)

- What convinced you it was a good idea to adopt this behavior?

- Ask to understand how this pattern/action has been helpful to you over the years.

- Has it ever been helpful to be excessively critical of yourself?

- Are you willing to extend kindness and respect to yourself even though you have this behavior?

- Consider the possibility that you may have this behavior for the rest of this lifetime. Notice how that makes you feel.

Now, ask your MTLOs to empower you to see how you can be useful to others. Invite them to clarify how you can love and share with others despite this unpleasant pattern. Ask for their help so you can accept yourself just the way you are today.

Close the Records and make some notes.

Seeking & Finding the Light in Ourselves & Others

We talk a lot about finding the Light in ourselves and others in the Records. What does this really mean, and how do we do it? Spiritual Light is expressed as positive human traits. People who are full of Light are aware of their inner Divine Spark and tend to be loving, kind, patient, and/or generous. They do not have literal beams of light emanating from them, but we may feel understood and accepted in their presence. When looking for the Light in an Akashic Records reading, we are searching for a person's positive, loving qualities. When spiritual Light connects with a person, that Light immediately converts into love. The best way to identify the Light in another is to search for the unique ways they express love. As we recognize and name these qualities, we begin to register the Light impressions converted into their loving energy.

Our ultimate opportunity is to love ourselves—to accept and understand the choices we make and the actions we take. Let yourself be convinced that you have always done your best, no matter how things turned out. Everyone is born with unique gifts, talents, and abilities. Your positive human qualities are not a mystery or a secret! Your human self is a treasury of spiritual riches expressed in ordinary ways! A significant benefit of spiritual awakening is that we consciously allow the Light of Life to use us, even though we are imperfect human beings. Our flaws and limitations do not prohibit the Light from shining through us for our own happiness and that of others. Even in human form, we can give and receive love. Perfection is not required!

The next two exercises—one simple and the other a bit more complex—are designed to amplify the Light of Life. Give them a try!

EMPOWERMENT EXERCISE #6

Seeking & Finding Your Light

Open your Records. Explore the following question, feeling free to ask for clarification: What are my unique gifts, talents, and abilities, and what are the best ways to use them at this point in my life?

Close the Records and pause to make some notes.

Next, we will do an exercise in your Records to center into the reality of who you are. I will invite you into the cave of the heart, a sacred space within each human body, which is the intersection point of the heart of the Universe and our relationship with the world. It is a safe, incorruptible place to observe our feelings, thoughts, and motivations. When I invite people to go within, this is where they naturally go. Consider the heart's cave as the energetic convergence of the personal, the communal, and the Universal. Here we go!

EMPOWERMENT EXERCISE #7
Centering in the Cave of Your Heart

Using the Pathway Prayer Process, open your Records. Take your place. Open your awareness to being here, right now. Plant yourself here. Bring to mind the Truth that the Universe has saved a place for you and that, at this very moment, you are sitting in that space.

Settling in, open up to the connection you have with the Earth. Let the planet hold you up. You are standing on layer upon layer of civilizations, your lifetimes, and the lifetimes of all others. Inspired human growth and expression in every area of life surrounds you—all generated to support you in this lifetime so that you may successfully bring your Soul's Purposes to life.

Direct your awareness into the cave of your heart—the crossroads of your multidimensional spiritual self and your countless human identities over time, and the unlimited contributions others have made to you simply through shared experiences and ideas. Settle into this space. Now, peer out of your back body to observe all the people lining up to support you in this life. Everyone you have ever known is gathering to encourage you to be your most authentic self in this Incarnation.

Now, expand your awareness to your left and right. Congregating here are your traveling companions from all lifetimes—all unique, all equal—shoulder to shoulder. You have made your way over continents, lifetime after lifetime. And now again, in this lifetime. From within the cave of your heart, look upward through the inner Pillar of Light, and out past your crown to the space approximately 18 inches above the crown of your head, the Soul level. Here are all Beings of Light assembled to shine your way—some very familiar, others totally unknown but all-loving, dedicated to you and your unfolding, lighting up your next right steps, lifetime after lifetime.

Again, redirect your attention, looking forward to the future. Whether the next 10,000 years or the next 30 minutes, be open to where your attention rests. There is a pathway to your ideal future, expressing all the love within you, sharing insights and wisdom you have been cultivating throughout the ages, contributing to the well-being of others in so many different ways. Take a moment to consider the spiritual potential of your awakening, loving yourself and all others without exception for all eternity. Full of love, we are each compelled to express it. It cannot be contained. We live many times simply to share all the love in our hearts.

Now, in your mind's eye, take a stand. You are a radiant point of Light in a field of radiant points of Light. Together, we become a bridge of Light composed of awakening humans aware of their spiritual identity and shining the way.

And so, for now, we leave this be. Close your Records using the Prayer. Pause to make some notes.

STRENGTHENING YOUR SKILLS

Principles & Protocols

Let's explore some foundational **Principles and Protocols** so we can resolve significant life challenges. Every reading offers "Energy Healing" in the Records. Energy moves on the formed word. The most powerful words are spoken, then written, and finally, thought. Energy also moves when we describe the answers to the questions we raised—whether our own or those of our client. Old patterns fracture when the Truth is spoken, opening the way for freedom from limitation. Our challenge is to describe what we encounter, addressing our client's concerns as we seek and find the Light in every difficulty.

Energy Healing in the Akashic Records is based on a primary spiritual paradox: the perfection of the infinite Soul and the simultaneous imperfection of the finite mortal human. Due to its expansive, inclusive nature, the Record has ample space to hold this paradox in its entirety. Based on the **Akashic Assumption** that every person is spiritually perfect—whole, well, and complete—there is never any need to send energy or pull energy away from anyone. Each individual has the ideal "amount" of energy within them, although, at times, they may forget this Truth. The issue is never whether someone has sufficient energy; the issue is whether they are aware that they do indeed have enough energy to live their life. As Practitioners, we are not bestowing healing but rather become the "allower" of healing, recognizing the reality of what is now and has always been true.

The Akashic understanding of acceptance is different from approval. With acceptance, there is a recognition of the presenting reality without any negative or positive opinions. Within the Akashic Field, this acceptance ignites a release of stuck ideas and behaviors. With acceptance, we initiate the release process, which happens quite naturally since our negative judgments cause stuckness in thought and action. Within the Akasha, we recognize that the goal of healing is to become more joyfully useful to ourselves and others. We acknowledge and allow goodness to flow. Perfection is not the goal; fulfilling usefulness is our intention. The purpose of all spiritual healing is to experience, express, and enjoy the love within.

The healing sequence in the Records is energy first, information second. While information is exciting, it does not always have the presence or force necessary to inspire change. That is why energy is more important than information. Energy Healing happens in the Records when the Practitioner knows the ultimate Truth of the goodness at the core of their client—that this individual has always taken the most loving action possible at every given moment, no matter the outcome. When the Practitioner is clear about this within the Records, the client more easily recalls their value and goodness. The Practitioner does not give the client healing but rather remembers the Truth so that the person being read can recall the Truth for themselves. The client has temporarily forgotten their Soul's perfection. The issue is awareness of well-being, not restoring it.

Roles & Responsibilities

Here are the **Roles and Responsibilities** of the Practitioner:

- The Practitioner is 100 percent responsible for the shift. Put no pressure on the client. If we "get" the Truth about the client, then they will, too. If we do not register their ultimate value, they cannot get it either.

• Our work is to seek and find the Light and good in everyone, no matter what appearances suggest.

• Light is identifiable by positive, good, noble, honorable human qualities and traits. We seek the most loving attributes in our clients no matter what difficulty they are embroiled in.

• We have the sacred opportunity to "fall in love" with each client—to recognize and understand them from the unconditionally loving perspective of the Akasha.

Three Levels of a Reading

There are **Three Levels of Every Reading**:

Level One: The Story
Level Two: Causes and Conditions
Level Three: Soul-Level Truth

LEVEL ONE: THE STORY

Describe the difficulty/issue: What is happening? What are the consequences? Avoid labels as you describe the problem's qualities, actions, and results. The problem may be a troublesome situation the client is trying to resolve or a challenge in manifesting their life dream. The Practitioner's role is to understand and accept how it is for the client to be having this experience, which is best done this way: *Listen. Accept. Allow.*

LEVEL TWO: CAUSES AND CONDITIONS

Explore the true nature of the difficulty. First, consider the point of origin: when, where, and why did it begin? Then search out, identify, and verbalize the positive reasons for all the client's choices, decisions they've arrived at, and actions they've performed. What convinced the client that this (selection/action) was in their best interest? Know that the choices and actions of the client were their optimal option, or they would have made different selections! Look for contributing factors: Past Lives, family of origin, ancestors, etc. The Practitioner's role is to recognize how the client's choice was a good idea at the time. Learn how the unfolding was the best possible option for the client.

LEVEL THREE: SOUL-LEVEL TRUTH

Here we "fall in love" with the client. Answer this question for yourself as a Practitioner: "How do I love my client even though they are having this unfortunate experience?" Be convinced of the lovable essence of the client, no matter what. Consider how the client can love, share and enjoy—even amid hardship. There is nothing that can extinguish the loving essence of your client. There is nothing they can do and nothing anyone else can do to them; it's simply impossible.

At each Level of the Reading: Check yourself for judgments, negative reactions, and opinions. Know yourself and ask for help in the Records as you move through the levels. Your acceptance and understanding as a Practitioner initiate transformation in the client. Watch to see if you are trying to "force" an idea or "insist" on change. Personal attachment to a particular outcome blocks the transformation.

Do you have a challenge you are ready to transform? Take it into the next Empowerment Exercise using the three-level approach.

EMPOWERMENT EXERCISE #8
Transforming a Significant Life Issue

Identify the biggest challenge in your life right now: a personal relationship, your career, health, money, family of origin, or creative self-expression. Open your Records following the protocol of the Pathway Prayer Process.

Begin with *Level One: The Story.* Describe the difficulty. What is the problem, and what are the consequences? Can you listen with an open mind? Can you accept that you have this issue?

Next is *Level Two: Causes and Conditions.*

- When did this begin? What was happening? Why did you start this behavior? What convinced you it was in your best interest to adopt this behavior? What were the contributing factors? Family patterns? Consider past lifetimes.

- What is the true nature of your difficulty? For example, what may look like a financial problem could be rooted in resentment toward authority. On the other hand, your difficulty may be exactly as it seems.

- Can you accept and have compassion for yourself even though you have this problem? Do you understand why you have this? Does this make good sense to you? Did you have any other options? Can you understand the good reasons you found your way into this difficulty?

- Now for the turbo-charged healing question: *Can you love, understand, and respect yourself even though you have this problem?*

Finally, we reach *Level Three: the Soul-Level Truth.*

- Notice that even the most horrible, tragic event you've ever experienced hasn't destroyed the love at the core of your being.

- Observe that you continue to love and share, participate, contribute, and even enjoy your life even in the middle of the worst situation.

- Nothing can obliterate the love that you are—nothing you do, and nothing anyone else does to you. You are a loving, infinite, unlimited, unstoppable being!

- Consider and be convinced that who you are is perfect at this time—no matter what.

Close your Records. Pause to make notes.

A NOTE FOR PRACTITIONERS

When you are doing your work in the Records, either for yourself or on behalf of another, you will not take the session apart in this way (the Three Levels). It is only for our learning that we do this. I want you to know what happens within a reading, what you can expect, and how to move from one level to another. That way, you will be much more comfortable in the Records, no matter what issues are addressed. Your comfort empowers your ability to recognize core issues and appropriate solutions in the Records. Now that you have clarity about the process of supporting your growth as an **Akashic Records Practitioner** and an idea of the Three Levels of every reading, we can move on to more powerful uses of the Akashic Records: Clearing Unwanted Ancestral Patterns and Reconciling Past Lives.

LESSON SEVEN

CLEARING UNWANTED ANCESTRAL PATTERNS

From an Akashic point of view, the primary purpose of the Soul's journey as human is to experience and express unconditional love for self, others, and all of creation. This perspective assumes that all of humanity is an expression of the Divine Reality. This is critical when considering freedom from limiting ancestral patterns for Karmic liberation, one of your Soul's Purposes.

We mentioned Karma before, but let's reconsider this vital pattern. Simply put, Karma is cause and effect, action/reaction, action/consequence. It is perfectly normal, natural, and predictable. However, we can run into trouble with this process when we apply our negative opinions, assessments, and judgments of ourselves, others, or the causes or effects of the Karmic pattern. When we meet the Karmic cycle with our negative condemnation, the pattern becomes stuck and repeats itself. Our unresolved judgments impact the cycle, causing it to stick. These patterns persist until we make peace with ourselves, others involved, and the causes and effects we are experiencing.

Freedom is a condition we all desire to varying degrees. Certainly, concerning painful Karmic patterns, we want freedom very much!

We achieve freedom by accepting and appreciating our choices in adopting a particular pattern. While it can seem counterintuitive that the path to expanding our freedom is accepting conditions we do not like, it is true. Every pattern is positive at the point of selection, or we would have chosen another option. Without exception, every pattern is supportive while we need it. It only becomes limiting or restricting when we outgrow it. Our awareness that the pattern is holding us back signals us to let it go.

Let's look at what is occurring spiritually with our family of origin. All Souls—in partnership with the Divine—choose family groups to accelerate their growth and transformation. Our personal choice of family is "for us," not "for them," which raises powerful questions: How do I love myself in their presence? How do I express myself in their presence? All family groups dissolve when every member is at peace with the others, accepting themselves and each other exactly as they are. This does not mean that everyone likes or enjoys one another. Peace comes from acceptance, simply recognizing the reality of the strengths and weaknesses of each family member and not trying to make anyone change.

In our next exercise, we will be visiting an inner Akashic dimension known as the **Zone of Choice**, the space from which we make significant choices. We make decisions in this realm about our identity and our family of origin, in partnership with the Ultimate Reality and the support of our MTLOs.

EMPOWERMENT EXERCISE #9
Finding Freedom from Limiting Ancestral Patterns

Open your Records using the Pathway Prayer Process. As you adjust to the Akashic Atmosphere, describe it. What qualities do you find here? What are the characteristics of this dimension? Expand your awareness, so you get a sense of residing in the loving company of your MTLOs.

Now, ask your MTLOs to facilitate your transition to the Zone of Choice. You may have a sense of traveling either up or down; either way is acceptable. Next, locate a place to stand within the Zone. It can be whatever you like; just find a location where you can "park" yourself for this segment of our work. Once situated, take a moment to focus on the qualities of the Zone of Choice. Normally, it is more intense and potent than our Records at large.

Now is the time to ask your MTLOs to assist you in connecting with the space and time when you chose your family of origin for this lifetime. You will not travel anywhere; rather, you will simply sense a slight shift in perception, as if you are connecting with another time and place, like opening a door or a window to a sliver of a past event that you recognize.

Begin by opening up to the matter of your Soul in partnership with the Divine, aided by your MTLOs. This is a customary connection, a transaction occurring in between every lifetime. Notice your family, relatives, parents. See their flaws, shortcomings, and any unresolved issues as well as their virtues, strengths, and exceptional qualities. Observe all the heroic work they have accomplished over scores of lifetimes. As you observe them, notice what emerges as the most compelling reasons you selected them out of all of the families available at that time.

- What do you recognize is possible for you by being with them?

- What were your intentions for being with them?

- What were your expectations?

- How did you expect life to unfold while you were with them?

- How can you grow and transform due to being in this family?

- How are they helping you become your best, most loving self?

Open your heart to the loving choice you made to be in this family. This was a brilliant choice on your part so you could become a more loving person due to being with them. Now, let this exercise go, and we will move on to another matter in the Zone of Choice.

Bring to your attention a pattern of thought or behavior that you share with your ancestors, which causes you difficulty at this point in your life. Describe the pattern. What do you do or avoid doing? Make a note of the consequences of this pattern. When you enact this pattern of behavior, what happens? What are the results? Ask your MTLOs when you adopted this pattern. You will not get a specific date, just a general or approximate time frame. Generally speaking, where were you? It may be a particular place, or it may be a region of the world or a particular environment, like a farm or small island. (It will not be a regular place you can find on a map.) What was happening? You made this choice to adopt this way of behavior for some very good reasons. What was going on that moved you to investigate some options for responding? How was this behavior a solution to a problem you were facing? You selected this specific behavior because it was a good idea at the time. What made you think it was a good choice for you?

Can you see how it was your best choice at the time? If you cannot recognize this fact, ask your MTLOs to help you. Make a note of how this pattern was helpful to you then. What convinced you it was a good idea to retain this pattern? See how you have grown as a result of having this pattern. If you have this pattern for the rest of your life, are you willing to love and respect yourself with it? Can you extend kindness and respect to yourself today while you still have this pattern? Are you willing to participate in life even though you have this perceived imperfection?

Ask your MTLOs to facilitate the shift from the Zone of Choice to the Akasha at large. You will travel the opposite way that you entered. Readjust to the spaciousness of the Akasha at large.

Close the Records. You may want to pause to make some notes.

RECONCILING PAST LIVES

I n this next segment, we will address the issue of Past Lives and the impact they have had on us through time. Everyone is seeking deep inner peace. Resolving ancient fears and resentments can liberate us today, igniting the love we carry in our hearts and initiating the flow of the unconditional love within.

We see Karma, the cause-and-effect cycle, as a natural part of our journey: we think thoughts, followed by actions that produce results. It is the way of Life here on this planet. Stuck Karma is a different matter, characterized by repetitive actions that stubbornly refuse to change, without regard for our necessity or wishes. They seem to be held in place by our unresolved self-judgment. We carry our negative opinions about ourselves from one lifetime to another until we make peace with them by accepting, releasing, and loving our imperfect selves in other times and places. Remember: acceptance facilitates release. A spiritual paradox is that accepting who we have been in different times and places, although imperfect, is the key to dissolving stuck patterns of behavior.

It may seem like we are upset about what others have done to us and the terrible things that happened to us in other places. This is true but incomplete. Other people may have acted in horrible ways to cause us immense harm, suffering, and grief. And we likely have done the same to others. We do not prefer to engage in hateful behavior, but it is a fundamental aspect of humanity.

From the Akashic point of view, everyone is always making optimal choices based on their needs and understanding of what will expand their experience of being loved and feeling safe. It may be that eliminating another person is one individual's best solution to a problem they face. This is an unfortunate action flowing from the intention of producing a positive result. While our instinct is to blame others, that does not inspire peace of mind or heart. We are invited to consider our part in every transaction. All power for transformation and healing always resides within us. Ask: What is my part? Who was I in this situation? Was I a victim? Was I a perpetrator? How do I love myself when I have been a victim? How do I love myself when I have been a predator?

Keep in mind that these exercises in Ancestral Clearing and Past Lives are only for your use as a Practitioner. If you can accept the events your client experienced and understand their valid reasons for choices they made and then, no matter what happened, love them unconditionally, you will ignite healing and transformation. Never insist that a client love themselves; it is counterproductive. Instead, the Practitioner's challenge is to unconditionally love and appreciate the client, to "Judge Not," thus honoring the Akashic Absolutes (*Fear Not, Judge Not*, and *Resist Not*).

Access this realm of Past Lives through present-day difficulties. We can only connect with a past life in the present! We do not go to the past; instead, we make a conscious connection with it in the present moment in time. The Akashic Record is not a "fishpond" of Past Lives but rather a reservoir for our empowerment, not entertainment. We unlock this realm by exploring today's difficulties, asking "when" or for the "point of origin" of the problem. If it is a past life issue, then that will be revealed. We do not need to know the entire story of the past life, simply the moment of a significant decision, the contributing factors, and the other identifying markers in a general way.

We want to know: Who? (relevant identity information); When? (approximately); and Where? (what region).

Our opportunity with Past Lives is to love who we have been in other times and places. It is consistent with the path of empowerment laid out in the Records for us to learn unconditional love through our lifetimes. Now, let's do an Empowerment Exercise to learn how this healing happens.

EMPOWERMENT EXERCISE #10
Reconciling Past Lives, Transcending Karma & Unleashing Unconditional Self-Love

Open your Records using the Pathway Prayer protocol. Begin by adjusting to the Akashic Atmosphere, recognizing this dimension's particular qualities and characteristics. Become aware of the loving support of your MTLOs.

Bring to mind a troubling issue you have in your life now. It can be about intimate relationships, your career, family of origin, finances, health, or creative self-expression. Maybe it's a grievance about yourself or something you do/not that causes you distress in this lifetime. Describe your behavior.

In your mind's eye, use your imagination to set up a Pillar of Light about an arm's length in front of you. Do this quickly, with the idea that it is anchored at the heart of the Earth, extending through the planet, the atmosphere, and beyond. Use this Pillar as a viewing station. Now, connect yourself to this Pillar with a single beam of light coming from your heart, linking you together. All you need to do is think of this, and it is so.

Ask your MTLOs to help you identify who you were in another time and place when you chose to adopt this behavior. See who you were, your gender, your social status in a general way. Were you involved in an occupation? What was your family configuration? Change has been slow on Earth so look more for the era than an exact date. Where were you—just a general sense of location. What region? Can you sense the climate? Do you have a feel for the region or certain geography? This feeling is more important than identifying a precise place. And now, what happened? What occurred to motivate you to select this behavior? Something always precedes a significant selection. What happened? Are there other options you could have chosen? Can you see that your choice was your best possible option at the time?

Can you open your heart to who you were when you made this selection? Ask your MTLOs to empower you to have compassion for who you were and the choices you made. Extend love to yourself. Invite who you were into your heart. Escort this person across the bridge into your heart space. Make room for this individual; you are already related, so this is not a stranger. Welcome them home in a way that is meaningful for you.

Let the Light Pillar collapse. Close the Records and make some notes.

You are doing great! We have one more exercise before pausing for another self-evaluation. I think you are going to enjoy immersing yourself in the Akashic Atmosphere.

EMPOWERMENT EXERCISE #11
Embodying the Consciousness of the Akasha

Open your Records using the Pathway Prayer Process. Take a few moments to settle into the Akashic Atmosphere. Make a note of the qualities you recognize: compassion, kindness, wisdom, patience, appreciation, and any other attributes of love you can identify. While the Akashic Atmosphere is always loving, the specific way love is expressed changes to meet our needs. Notice the dominant qualities today. Open your awareness to the presence of your profoundly compassionate MTLOs. Sense their presence; know that you are the most important focus of their attention, worthy of the guidance and wisdom they have for you.

In your mind's eye, set up your Pillar of Light approximately an arm's length in front of you. Do this quickly with the power of your thought. Simply think of it being there and so it is. Anchor this Pillar into the heart of the Earth, bring it up through the planet and out beyond this dimension, into the cosmos as far as your awareness allows, then let it go where it will.

Now, ask your MTLOs to empower you to see yourself as they know you. Place yourself in the Pillar of Light and adjust your perception to align with the Soul-level point of view of the Akasha. You may become aware of love radiating from your core or a particular characteristic that is your signature expression of kindness and respect. Additionally, you may get a sense of the love and appreciation they have for you.

Now, expand the Pillar. Bring into your Pillar of Light a handful of your favorite people. They could be your spouse, children, best friends, or others. Make room in the Pillar for all of you to be together in this loving space. Now, sense them in the Light of the Akasha. Open up to the deep and effervescent love shared by this group.

At this time, expand the Pillar again and bring in a few people you do not like. You may dislike them a little, or you may have strong feelings of anger and contempt for them. These feelings may be for good reasons or no reason at all. Now, ask your MTLOs to help you see them, to know them as they are known in the Light of Truth. Adjust your vision to perceive them as Souls: infinite, eternal, immortal beings of love. There's no need to do anything to them or send them light. Simply look for the love shining through these imperfect individuals. As we all are.

Now is the time to expand the Pillar again. Bring the entire human family into your Pillar of Light. Include all the people from every race, continent, religion, socioeconomic group, region, and any other category that seems to separate us. Exclude no humans; all means all. Let yourself get a sense of the whole of humanity being seen and known in the Light of Truth. Open your heart to the love emanating from this group, transcending differences and distinctions, and the love activated within you. Let the love flow back and forth.

Open your heart now and take the Earth and all of its inhabitants into your loving heart space. Let yourself love all life forms existing here on the planet. Hold them close. And let yourself be loved in return. Allow your Pillar of Light to dissolve. And so, for now, we leave this be.

Close the Records and make some notes.

PAUSE FOR SELF-REFLECTION

Now is an important time in your journey, ideal for reflecting on your progress. Take a few minutes to think back to when you first began. Notice how your connection with your Records has grown. You have made great strides, no doubt. At this point, you have a solid foundation for working in the Records—for yourself and others. Improvement comes with practice. Don't be shy about practicing as much as you can. You will only get better, helping yourself and others as you improve. The Universe will only send you people you can help, so never worry about who reaches out to you for assistance. In our perfect Universe, you are sure to find others looking for the gifts, talents, and abilities you have to share.

THE FIVE-POINTED STAR & THE INNER ASCENSION MATRIX

A significant spiritual challenge of our age is this: How can we be spiritually awake and engage effectively in the world simultaneously? We are spiritual and physical, unified, nondual beings. Since the core of our being is spiritual Light and love, we want to express that in our lives. A sincere desire of those of us on the spiritual path is to consciously live Soul-led lives that demonstrate the Truth of who we are. The challenge is: how do we do this?

Let's keep in mind some basic ideas about the nature of Light and our relationship to it. The nature of Light is simultaneously radiant and magnetic. As we clear obstructions to our inherent radiance, the Light shines through us, as us, out into the world. And, at the same time, the Light, by its magnetic property, naturally draws to us that which is ours, bringing to us whatever we need to bring our Soul's Purposes to life.

Our responsibility is to clear obstructions to the Light. We do not create Light; Light is already created. But we have an opportunity to increase our personal radiance/magnetism by resolving old ideas, relinquishing blockages, and restoring a relationship of respect and admiration with ourselves.

All obstructions or blockages are solidified negative judgments. Releasing these blockages requires accepting that we are stuck, identifying the negative opinion, judgment, or condemnation we have about the particular issue; recognizing the positive value of our prior choices; and embracing the fact that there were valid reasons for our decisions. Finally, our acceptance facilitates release and liberates us from archaic patterns to fully accept the situation and our part in it. Let's examine the Five-Pointed Star to learn more about being spiritually awake as we engage in the world. This is another basic practice, which we will revisit at each level of learning.

My journey, like yours, has had specific chapters of discovery and growth. I wrote about each segment in my previous books. The first, *How to Read the Akashic Records*, was all about the method, the Record, and its applications. In my second book, *Healing Through the Akashic Records*, I explored personal healing. When my personal healing was sufficient, I ventured into the world. Challenged by spiritual sensitivity, I explored my Records for help. Working in my Records ,striving to understand this dilemma and discover a good solution, I was shown a group of Pillars of Light surrounding the central core pillar within—each one required for effective, satisfying participation in the world. This experience was most unusual, as I rarely see images and had no idea what this could mean, so I asked for help. My MTLOs revealed each Pillar or concept to me, one at a time, and introduced the idea of connecting with their spiritual essence. Once everything was peaceful and harmonized, the inner Light at the center of my being could shine freely into the world with its magnetic radiance. This is true for all of us and led to *Discover Your Soul's Path Through the Akashic Records*.

The Five-Pointed Star

Five core concepts connect our inner Light to the outer world. Our effectiveness and happiness in our ordinary life are greatly enhanced when the link between our inner Light and outer expression is clear.

Each concept has spiritual and worldly dimensions, with Grace at the core. As we identify and align with the spiritual essence of each concept, power and Light flow. In order, the five concepts are:

1 Incarnation
2 Authority
3 Discipline
4 Responsibility
5 Commitment

Let's consider each one:

Incarnation: To be incarnate is to be a spirit in human form. To find success in this lifetime, you must make peace with your human self. *You* are the optimal agent for your Soul and its purposes in your evolution and the world. Who you are as a person is your Soul's first and best choice!

Authority: Harmonious, productive human living always involves engagement with human authority. It is just a fact for humans here on Earth. There is always an authority greater than we are: a parent, a boss, or even the government. It is not personal; it is the way the world works. Making peace with ourselves in this arena is our access to aliveness and power. The perfect power of the Divine is transmitted to us and through us as imperfect human beings. And while each of us is the author of our personal universe, no one of us is God of *the* Universe. As we resolve our issues with authority, we take our rightful place in the Circle of Life as both givers and receivers of authority.

Discipline: It is so easy to confuse discipline and punishment, but they are very different. Discipline is from the word "disciple," which means "to listen." A discipline is any action that empowers our ability to listen and hear the inner voice of Truth. It is not punishment (an attempt to stop a person from behaving in a way that makes others uncomfortable). With appropriate disciplines, we develop supportive structures through which the energy of Life flows to us and from us out into the world.

Responsibility: When it comes to responsibilities, the first distinction we need to make is between true and false. True responsibilities to ourselves and others serve as a crucible for transformation, inviting us to let go of limiting patterns and develop inspired patterns for living. True responsibilities are the avenue through which we transform into the best version of ourselves. False responsibilities are ego-based, fearful, and drain or distract us from our Soul's Purposes.

Commitment: Commitment is the quality that enables us to hang on, to stay the course when life gets difficult. Every path has its treasures embedded in it, but we can only access them after we commit to the path. To turbo-charge your path, commit to it—and you will experience greater inspiration and more fulfillment.

Let's do an exercise in your Records to explore these five important spiritual concepts.

EMPOWERMENT EXERCISE #12
The Five-Pointed Star

Open your Records following the Pathway Prayer protocol. Now, settle into the loving, empowering space that is the Akasha. These are your Records, and by now, you are quite familiar with this place: it is a sacred space reserved for you. Get comfortable.

With the guidance of your MTLOs, direct your attention to the Pillar of Light at the center of your being. Start at the root and move up the trunk of your body and out the crown of your head. Find a place within the Pillar to center yourself; it can be in the region of your heart or lower in your belly. Whatever feels best to you is the correct place to be. Sit within the Pillar and look out beyond it, through yourself and out into the world.

Now, direct your attention or your gaze forward. Have your MTLOs guide you to recognize a Pillar of Light directly in front of you but still within your body. It is smaller than the Pillar you are sitting in. This is the Pillar of Incarnation. Take a moment to review your relationship with the particulars of this life. Let yourself recall problems you have had with yourself. How about with your family? Our intent is to make peace with who we are in the lifetime in which we find ourselves. Consider the possibility that who you are as a person is ideal for demonstrating and expressing your Soul's essence. And the person you are is not an accident but instead is your Soul's first and best choice in this lifetime. Now, let this go.

Next, move your awareness to the right front of your body, to the Pillar of Authority. Reflect on your general relationship to authority. Notice your standard response to authority. Do you tend to reject or judge authority? Are you usually fearful of authority? Ask whether you are willing to allow imperfect authority figures like parents to transmit the energy of perfect authority. Am I willing to be an imperfect authority to others? Let this go.

Let's redirect awareness to our back body, the right side, looking out to the Pillar of Discipline. What is your automatic reaction to the idea of discipline? Do you confuse punishment with discipline? Do you reject it altogether in favor of being a free spirit? Do you tend to over-disciplining under-disciplining yourself? Is there a pattern of behavior that would quiet your mind and empower you to hear the wisdom of the voice of Truth within? Let's leave this be now.

Next, focus on the left side of your back body, looking out to the Pillar of Responsibility. Note your general response to responsibility. Observe your pattern of true and false responsibilities in this life. True responsibilities transform us into our best selves. False responsibilities deplete us. Most of us have a combination of tendencies. Make note of your pattern. Consider your level of willingness to be transformed by your true responsibilities in this lifetime. Let yourself embrace your true responsibilities and the opportunities they hold. Let this go.

At this point, let your awareness travel to the left side of your front body, gazing out to the fifth Pillar of Light, Commitment. Notice your default; do you avoid commitment or become engulfed in it? Ask your MTLOs if there is a commitment you can take on at this time in your life. Is there a commitment that will activate the power of your path? Remember, your path can only nurture you once you commit.

Now, bring your awareness back into the central Pillar of Light, the Pillar of Grace. Find a place to rest. Observe the clarity of the Pillars. Notice the Infinite Light at the center of your being shining out into the world. There is no need to send Light; simply allow it to find its way through and beyond you as it radiates. At the same time, the Light magnetizes what you need to bring your Soul's Purposes to life. Stand as a lighthouse in your world so that you can be easily recognized by everything seeking you.

And so, for now, we let this be. Close the Records. If you wish, you can make some notes.

The Inner Ascension Matrix

This exciting segment of the work prepares you to go out into the world as a Practitioner. To ascend is to rise above. It is a lofty concept but very simple to activate. Ascension is not literal but personal and spiritual. It can happen for you here and now. There's no need to wait for anyone else! Ascension is a natural result of our expanding awareness. We naturally rise above our circumstances and live in the realm of unlimited possibilities as our awareness of spiritual Truth expands. It is an expected consequence: by engaging in activities that support our alignment, encouraging authentic self-expression, we naturally ascend.

Let's begin with understanding a matrix: a situation or condition within which something else originates or develops, mathematically composed of three columns. Ours are Gratitude, Grace, and Generosity. Each has a role to play in our Ascension Matrix:

- Gratitude provides momentum.

- Grace accelerates the process; it is the catalyst.

- Generosity gives velocity so we can move forward horizontally and vertically simultaneously.

Now, let's examine them one at a time.

Gratitude facilitates momentum. It is cumulative; it gathers and retains, building on itself. With Gratitude, we recognize the positive value of something and actively appreciate it. It contributes to "escape speed"—the speed required to move to another level. So, if we are in one situation and want to be better situated, we need more escape speed to depart that circumstance and enter an improved condition. Gratitude accelerates our escape speed so that we can improve our station in life. Our goal is to be mostly grateful, most of the time. As humans, we are not expected to be 100 percent grateful 100 percent of the time. Mostly grateful, most of the time is the key to our transformation. Even amid terrible experiences, we can find something for which to be grateful. But our Gratitude must be real; the Universe does not appreciate false Gratitude. Do not bother pretending you are thankful when you are not. (Although I may dread and loathe my job, I can appreciate the paycheck, my work friends, the hours, etc.)

Grace is the catalyst of the Ascension Matrix. It initiates or accelerates the change while maintaining its identity. Grace's disposition is to be helpful and merciful with a spirit of goodwill. Grace is recognized as an aspect of the Divine, a state of being perfected. It is almost a magical quality, bringing out the best in everything. Grace is constant, unwavering, permanent, eternal, infinite, and fully present. We cannot manufacture Grace, but we can seek and find it and then recognize it. When we behold Grace, this amplifies it: the more we are aware of Grace, the more it seems to expand. Our awareness of Grace intensifies Grace. While we cannot generate Grace, our appreciation of this "sacred quality" strengthens it.

Generosity gives us buoyancy and liftoff; it provides velocity. It enables us to move forward and upward at the same time. Giving is a process of liberation: as we give, we become buoyant, we ascend. Intention is a good beginning but giving is taking action, making a choice. It is deliberate, love in action, which is transformational for the giver. As we give what we value, we are liberated and lightened up. We are free. It is our birthright to give freely because we have been given so much.

Now let's do an **exercise** to explore your inner Ascension Matrix.

EMPOWERMENT EXERCISE #13

The Inner Ascension Matrix

Open your Records using the Pathway Prayer Process. Center yourself in the depths of your Records. This is your sacred sanctuary, a
seat of honor and reverence for you and your Soul. Take your place.
Welcome the company of your MTLOs. Ask them to help you recognize how your awareness has been expanding since we started
working together. How has Grace been working as a catalyst in activating your Matrix? Where in your Matrix can you step in? What
is the point of ignition in your Matrix right now? All three components live inside you all the time, but sometimes it is easier to
connect with one or another.

Scan your inner Matrix: Gratitude, Grace, and Generosity. Where do
you sense an opening—perhaps Gratitude? Are you especially grateful
for something at this time: an insight, an experience, an understanding? Are you more thankful today than you were yesterday for some
aspect of your life?

Is there anything or anyone for whom you have more appreciation than
usual? Can you look to see if you can give time, attention, encouragement, or action to someone in the near future? Generous thoughts are
a good start, but they are only a beginning. To stimulate the full benefit
of Generosity, we have to give. What can you give and to whom? Is
there something you would like to do for another? Is there something
you would like them to have? Is there something you feel is valuable
that you can share with someone else?

What activates Grace is your witness. As you notice and acknowledge Grace, it gets stronger. Do you have an awareness that a special
protection or enhancement is showering down something significant
to you? Maybe you recognize that one area of your life is seamless,
effortless, and almost magical. Or there is a person in your life with
whom you share a marvelous connection. Consider your life and how
some parts are just wonderful no matter what transpires. To empower
Grace, to strengthen it, observe it. Give Grace the credit it deserves.

Now, look to see if there is an opening in your Matrix. As the Matrix within you gets activated, it becomes more powerful, so you can rise above the challenges of your life journey. Ask the MTLOs to help you see yourself from the level of ascension. What qualities distinguish you as an ascending being? What characteristics and traits come into focus as you ascend? Ask your MTLOs to help you see the positive impact your ascending consciousness has as you go about your daily life. Observe the valuable improvements in your life when you deliberately cultivate this altitude of awareness.

Consider your work, health, relationships, finances, and creative self-expression. Notice how they improve with your ascending consciousness. Have your MTLOs guide you to the space of ascending Souls who have gone before you. Notice how they have made room for you, saving you a place. Now, out of Generosity, open the path to those who follow, making room for all who seek a more meaningful life. Make it easy for them through your kindness, Generosity, and Gratitude.

Stand with the group of knowers: those who know the Truth, those who seek the Truth, those who enjoy the Truth, and those who live the Truth. Know yourself as a point of Light within a greater Light. A point of Light among legions of Light. Together, we are indeed the Light of the World. And for now, we leave this be.

Close your Records. If you like, pause and make some notes.

Congratulations! You have completed Level I. You are well on your way to becoming a Practitioner! Of course, there is always more to the journey, but it is best to take one step at a time. This may be a good time to pause to give yourself a chance to grow into all that you have been learning. Savor your expanding consciousness. Feel free to return to any of the exercises in this section for more practice.

LEVEL II

HEALING THROUGH THE AKASHIC RECORDS

evel II of the Akashic Records Teachings is an opportunity to increase your understanding of healing work in the Akashic Records and explore and experience practices to strengthen your foundation as an Akashic Records Practitioner. Here are many opportunities for you to delve into your issues for resolution—making it easier for you to become increasingly proficient in your practice, thereby developing your ability to do remarkable, effective, transformational work with others.

Our primary purpose at this Level is to transform our relationship with sustained wounds and injuries into sacred opportunities to embrace our Soul's perfection. We will learn the spiritual practice of unconditional self-love, revolutionizing our relationship with ourselves and others. Our relationships with others become an avenue for peace as we move from resentment to acceptance and find freedom from limiting patterns. We can then explore new levels of depth in our work with our ancestors and family relations, as well as in examining past life influences. Our focus is on healing ourselves first and then others, based on the principle that we can only transmit what we have experienced. After this, your work with others will be supercharged! We will clear away any obstructions to our awareness of the eternal, timeless Oneness with ourselves, others, and all of creation. We recognize that all of planetary Life is the physical expression of Divine Reality in our minds and hearts.

As is our practice, let's begin with a centering meditation. *You can also access a video of me guiding this meditation here: www.lindahowe.com /Akashic-Meditations.*

AKASHIC LIGHT MEDITATION II

Here and now, take this opportunity to settle into your place, wherever your body is physically situated. Each of us consciously occupies our very own unique place on this planet. Seat yourself squarely in your seat with your back straight, feeling comfortable and supported by your chair. Feel your bottom connected with your chair, the floor, the Earth.

Sitting here, notice that there is a space that you alone occupy. You share it with no other person—it's just yours. No other human being can take your place. You are the only you that has ever existed, that will ever be. Life has saved a place for you. You are the intentional, deliberate expression of Life as you.

Now, open your awareness to the space between your seat and the heart of the Earth. Imagine a beam of Light emanating from the core of the planet to you, supporting you as a person in the world. Let yourself get a sense of this remarkable support dedicated to you! This beam of Light extends from the heart of the Earth through you and beyond. This supportive ray of Light moves through you to approximately 18 inches above the crown of your head. Here is the place where your individual Soul becomes distinct from the One Soul that we all are. You never, ever separate from the whole, but your identity becomes individualized at this point.

Let your awareness travel up to this point. Peer up and over the point, opening up to this horizon of Light. Get a sense of the Infinite Light of Life seeking you out, finding you here and now. The Light moves toward you from all directions—behind, on both sides, even above you. This Light has been your constant companion since the inception of your Soul, leading you, guiding you, as you move along your Soul's journey as human throughout all your incarnations.

Now, bring your attention to your heart space, the cave of your heart, and let yourself rest here. As you do this, the Light follows you into your body. Light streams into you through your crown, effortlessly and elegantly filling you up, saturating every atom of your being—so that there's no more space within you.

At this point, open your heart center from the inside. Allow the Light to flow out in a stream, down into the Earth, finding its way to the core—along the way, meeting with streams of Light from everyone who has ever done this meditation—so together, we form a magnificent stream of Light anchored at the heart of the Earth. And then allow it to come up through the planet, through the layers of human consciousness in physical form—up through your location, out the ceiling, through the roof. Together, let's take this Pillar of Light to the edge of the consciousness of all students of the Akasha—as far as we can imagine. And from there, we let it go where it will.

Now, bring your attention back to your room. Notice your connection to this Pillar through your heart. Next, expand the Pillar to extend to each wall. Press it into the seams where the floor meets the walls and the walls meet the ceiling. Now we are set within a Pillar of Light perfectly calibrated to us, here and now. And from this place, we begin our work. And so, we do acknowledge the Forces of Light, asking for guidance, direction, and courage to know the Truth, as it is revealed for our highest good and the highest good of everyone connected to us.

Open your eyes and come into the room.

If it is safe to do so, light the Akashic Candle, a symbol of the Truth that there is a Light within and beyond you, illuminating your way. Keep this burning while you do this work. Carefully extinguish it when you are finished.

LESSON ONE

HEALING THROUGH THE AKASHIC RECORDS

My Healing Story

We have many things to discuss, but before tackling larger matters, I want to share a bit about myself and how *Healing Through the Akashic Records* came to exist. The material we are about to examine was brought to my attention at a critical time in my life. My son was a young, highly creative Soul, so I found myself challenged every day: striving to impart discipline and good behavior without crushing his spirit. At the same time, my father was dying a long, slow, painful death. I had high standards for myself and my behavior, which, unfortunately, I could not live up to—nor could anyone else.

As I dove into my Records, I asked for insight, guidance, and wisdom to deal with these simultaneous difficulties. Over some time, I recognized a remarkable patience, compassion, and understanding coming from my Records. It was amazing in the face of my imperfection—as if I could do no wrong! No matter my emotions or behavior, the Records kept returning to a simple message of acceptance, kindness, and respect. Soon, I realized that unconditional compassion was the message—

and the idea for my second book was born. It took some time for me to grow through all of the material, practices, and protocol. Applying the idea was a journey all its own—one with great results. Ultimately, I shared the teachings I was blessed with in *Healing Through the Akashic Records*.

It is important to remember that this work is specific to the Pathway Prayer Process to Access the Heart of the Akashic Records. For best results, please use that Prayer to open and close your Records (just as you learned in Level I).

Now that you know more about my connection to this material, reflect on your reasons for studying and what you hope to gain.

Tips for Success

I want to share some helpful ideas to support your success in this book. Our focus is on spiritual healing based on love. This book is about identifying and activating the love present in ourselves, no matter the condition of our bodies, minds, or emotions. We are not doctors and will not address, fix, or cure medical problems. However, you will come to understand the **Akashic Approach** to such difficulties, as well as strategies empowering your ability to ignite love in the presence of physical hardship. As a Practitioner, you will learn how to transform your relationship with conditions and experiences so that you can enjoy peace and freedom no matter what horrible things have happened in your lifetime.

Another critical distinction is healing "through" the Records, not "by" the Records. The Records are a body of energy and, as such, do not take any actions for or against us. They exist as a cross-section of Universal Heart, Mind, and Will. Engaging in this Field, you have the opportunity to identify the Truth of matters and initiate the process of letting go of old interpretations holding you back. Ultimately you will grow in peace and freedom, no matter what challenges you face in your life.

We live in times of global transformation made possible by the shift within individuals. As one person after another awakens to greater

Truth, the wave of awakening awareness sweeps each continent. These are our times. And your personal healing is vital to that wave. You are a unique individual, existing here and now to be useful to yourself and others. The gifts you carry are exactly what the world needs now. Global transformation invites us all to grow in spiritual maturity. A spiritually mature person recognizes the imperfections of being human and the perfection of the Soul at the same time. This fundamental paradox is held in the Records and within every one of us. We are infinite and finite, perfect and imperfect—and this is precisely the way it is meant to be.

Your commitment to this work and participation in the process will empower you to be more effective in your Records work, whether on your own or with others. This class accelerates your personal growth, enhancing your ability to assist other people. The good news is that your authentic giving fuels your ascension.

I know that you have a deep desire to accommodate ever-expanding states of Light. In order to do that, you are required to address your human vulnerabilities. The Light does not expect us to be perfect, only to be honest and not allow ourselves to withdraw from Life because we are flawed. In this class, you learn how to let the Light shine through you, as you, just the way you are—knowing that you are good enough and just what the world needs right now. Next, we will explore the nature, potential, and promises of the Akashic Records as an infinite spiritual resource.

Spiritual Fitness

Students often ask for the most efficient strategy to accelerate progress in their Records' practice. It is a paradox that the best way to strengthen your ability to accommodate spiritual Light is by fortifying your human instrument. The following practice is all about who you are as a person: an agent for Akashic Light while still in human form! We will practice empowering your spiritual fitness. The purpose of this exercise is to help you grow into greater intimacy and richness in your relationship with your Records. You can use it as a guide for your ever-deepening practice for spiritual illumination and inspiration. I recommend this as a regular practice to increase your spiritual fitness and prepare you to be the best Practitioner possible.

EMPOWERMENT EXERCISE #14
Spiritual Fitness

Open your Records following the protocol using the Pathway Prayer Process. Settle in and get comfortable within your Records. Open your awareness to the exceptionally kind, respectful presence of your MTLOs. Although you never see them, you can certainly get a felt sense of their presence and support.

Now, focus on the environment of your Records, known as the Akashic Atmosphere. As you get a sense of the Akashic Atmosphere, describe it to yourself. What are some of the qualities or characteristics of this sacred space? Overall, you are sure to detect loving qualities, but they always morph to become the precise characteristics we need at any given time. Can you recognize some of the ways the loving Akashic Atmosphere supports you today? It may be infused with patience, understanding, or even enthusiasm. Make a note of the traits you encounter.

At this time, direct your attention to yourself at the center of this space. Scan yourself, looking for the condition of your general well-being. Identify and describe it. Ask yourself how you are doing today and describe it as though answering a sincere friend. Share a general assessment of your well-being today.

Look now to your physical self, your body. How are you today? Describe the general state of your health. Identify specific strengths and weaknesses you may find. Most of us are a combination of positive and negative qualities. You may feel robust with some aches and pains or something similar. Go ahead and observe your physical condition. Ask your MTLOs for guidance about any physical challenge you have today. Although they will not intervene and correct any discomfort, they will provide insight, wisdom, or suggestions for you to apply concerning your physical health.

Now, consider your emotional state. Notice your feelings and name them. All emotions are acceptable. Whether you recognize anger, sorrow, fear, or myriad other emotions, know that these are all normal. Ask your MTLOs to empower you to recognize and receive any emotional support you need today. While they never deprive us of our emotions or change our feelings, our MTLOs are always available to help us cope with our emotional Truth. They may also have some recommendations about taking care of yourself, so you are emotionally sound today and on an ongoing basis.

Direct your attention to your thoughts and observe the types that arise today. They may be generating peace, tranquility, confidence, and composure. However, it is also possible that you are thinking thoughts activating fear and distress. You are the chooser of your thoughts. You have the power of selection when it comes to your thoughts, so choose wisely. Select ideas that you find nurturing and uplifting. It is common for human beings to need a boost to entertain more loving ideas. Ask your MTLOs for support in thinking loving thoughts as you go through your day today.

Now, look to this day, just this day. Review your plans for the day. There may be some pleasurable activities ahead, and others that are more difficult. No matter what you have planned, ask your MTLOs to assist you in meeting the day with confidence and compassion.

Finally, ask your MTLOs if they have a special, private message to inspire you for the day at hand. It may be a few words, a sentiment, or an image. It is just for you. Take that message and hold it in your heart. It will take root, grow, and become part of you as you do this.

Close your Records, reading the Closing Prayer out loud. Then, pause and make some notes.

LESSON TWO

CLEARING UNWANTED ANCESTRAL PATTERNS

C learing unwanted ancestral patterns is significant for those of us on the path seeking greater peace and freedom. Here, we are interested in clearing behaviors that interfere with our authentic self-expression and fulfillment. We share many patterns with our family groups that are helpful, so it is in our best interest to retain those. Clearing requires using a spiritual perspective for viewing our human selves, the point of view of unconditional love. With this point of view, we recognize and identify the loving intentions of every human being.

Akashic Assumptions

Let's review some foundational ideas for effective clearing, beginning with Akashic Assumptions for considering human behavior. From this perspective, every human being in existence is essentially good at their core. There are no exceptions to this assumption: everyone is good, even when their behavior is terrible. Each human being is always doing their best (even when their best is not nearly as good as they or anyone else wishes). And finally, every choice, decision, or selection made by any person at any time in any situation is motivated by a person's desire to expand their experience of being safe and loved. Sometimes these choices bring about terrible, troublesome results, but at the level of motive, the intention is geared toward a positive outcome for the chooser. This last point deserves repeating. From an Akashic perspective, every choice, every action is an effort to experience love. This idea applies even when the action results in harm or destruction. Every effort intends to secure a greater experience of love, peace, safety, and well-being. Understanding Akashic principles, especially Karma, makes a dramatic positive difference in Ancestral Clearing work, contributing to the permanent resolution of inherited ancestral patterns. (You may want to review what we learned about Karma in Level I.)

Now let's move on to healing unwanted ancestral patterns. Depending on where we are on the path, particular patterns may be causing us difficulty. Asking "What's in the way for me now?" will usually reveal the ancestral pattern. Sometimes it's as simple as overeating. Maybe the women in your lineage have trouble speaking up. Or there's an incessant gambling problem that can be traced back a few generations. Whatever the pattern of behavior, we know that whatever it is was the very best way to survive at the time. But now you may be wondering, "Maybe there's another way..."

The Akashic Realm

The Records are a perfect dimension for resolving ancestral complications for many reasons. As the cosmic memory of all humans over time, it makes sense to explore this realm to solve our difficulties. Additionally, the Akashic Realm is a unified field of consciousness containing all paradoxical ideas. (A paradox is when contrary or opposing ideas both seeming to be true exist within the same space.) The Records comfortably contain paradoxical ideas at different levels of existence. By working in your Records, you can more easily identify inherited patterns of consciousness detrimental to your growth and understand valid reasons for choices affecting you today. Ultimately, we have the option of aligning with the highest possibilities of our ancestral group and elevating desirable traits for the good of the human family.

Soul Groups

Your ancestors are those with whom you share consciousness, including both those on a Soul level and those to whom you are connected biologically. A **Soul Group** is a collection of people who share personal and universal Soul-level goals. We choose Soul Groups to promote our Soul-level awareness. It may seem that we select groups or families to assist them with their journeys. While that may come to pass, our choice is first and foremost based on facilitating our transformation. In a Soul Group, the entire group stays together over a series of incarnations until all group members accept all other group members. Everyone does not have to like one another, just respect each other. Your very first Soul Group is your family of origin. When you arrived here in this lifetime, you shared consciousness with your family. In some lifetimes, we grow away from our starting place; in other lifetimes, we do not grow very much at all. Notice your relationship with your family group, how it has evolved, and how it has stayed the same. There is no such thing as cutting cords to escape a Soul Group. Because we are all one, unified in Light and Truth, no amount of imaginary cord-cutting will sever the ties we have with one another. Instead, we have an incredible opportunity to love and respect ourselves—even when we are related to people we do not understand or appreciate, or who do not understand or appreciate us!

There are a few ways to join a family group; birth, adoption, marriage, and even friendship are all valid ways of entering familial groups. Divorce is a way to transition out of one group and into another. However, from the Records' point of view, freedom from a family group joined through marriage is most successful after you make peace with yourself for marrying that particular person in the first place. As you love and respect yourself for choices you made earlier in your life, you unleash your inner peace, and the divorce becomes anchored in harmony. This can be a helpful way to support yourself if you are going through a divorce process.

Many of us have a sense of responsibility to our ancestors. Sometimes this is clear, and at other times, vague. Ultimately, our responsibility is to unconditionally love and accept ourselves in their presence no matter how they receive or treat us. And to dignify everyone in the group by accepting them just the way they are, allowing them to be their authentic selves in our presence.

Before we do our next exercise in the Records, I want to remind you about the Zone of Choice. The Zone of Choice is an inner Akashic Realm, the space we visit in between incarnations. It is a sacred space where we partner with our MTLOs in cooperation with the Ultimate Reality to review the progress we are making on our Soul's journey as human and make selections supporting our unfolding and awakening in our upcoming lifetime. You are welcome to work in your Zone of Choice at any time—as long as you do so in concert with your MTLOs. Keep in mind that this realm is for you only because you have earned this privilege as a Practitioner. Recall that it is never helpful to use the Zone of Choice when reading with a client. It is unfair to yourself and your client to attempt to guide them into this realm. If you are working with a client addressing ancestral issues, you will be given ample resources on their behalf without entering their Zone of Choice.

Now let's do an exercise in our Records exploring our relations with our family of origin.

EMPOWERMENT EXERCISE #15

Exploring Family Relations in the Zone of Choice

Open your Records using the Pathway Prayer Process. Give yourself a chance to acclimate to the Akashic Atmosphere, an environment that you know by now to be characterized by welcome and warmth. In the company of your MTLOs, you can sense their dedication and support for you.

Placing yourself in the middle of your Records, ask for illumination about your relationship with your family of origin. In the inspired company of your MTLOs, ask for assistance identifying the traits inherited from both of your parents. Imagine your mother to the left and your father to your right. If you were adopted, include both birth parents (even if you've never met them) and the parents who raised you. Include them all and their positive and negative characteristics (naming as many as you possibly can).

Ask your MTLOs to help you to sense and understand:

- How you are linked to these people. What are the similarities? What are the differences?

- What are the positive gifts of being in this group?

- What are the responsibilities of being a member of this family group?

- What are the privileges of this membership?

- What are the Divine intentions and possibilities for this group?

- What are the shared Soul's Purposes for members of this group?

- Have your MTLOs give you a sense of your family group moving together over time and through space.

Ask your MTLOs to empower you to shift into the Zone of Choice (that space within the Akashic Field from which we make selections for upcoming incarnations, in partnership with the Divine, supported by our MTLOs). You may have a sense of being lifted or lowered; either way is acceptable. Pay attention to the direction you travel. As you shift into the Zone, find a place to stand and let yourself settle into this space. In the company of your MTLOs, ask these questions: Out of the family groups available, why did you select this set of parents? What was particularly appealing about them? What did they have that you wanted to learn or attain for yourself? What drew you to choose them over all possible parents? What were your intentions when you made this choice? What were your purposes? What were your expectations? How did you expect life to unfold while you were with them? Observe the differences between your expectations and the reality of your experience. How has being in this family helped you realize your Soul's Purposes? Ask for help to get a sense of the relationship between your Soul's Purposes and this family's choice.

We know that you are here to learn to love yourself unconditionally. Ask yourself how you can love yourself for choosing to be in this family. How can you love yourself in their company even if they don't understand or appreciate you? How can you dignify them by allowing them to be precisely the way they are in your presence?

Now, have your MTLOs help you return to your Records at large by retracing your steps. When you return, take a moment to enjoy the spaciousness of the Akasha at large. Let your new insights settle in. Close your Records. Pause and make some notes.

Transforming Family Relationships

In this next segment, we will focus on two important ideas for transforming our relationships with our family of origin. Do this while continuing to recognize and understand yourself within the Akashic Light, fueling your growth and development. First, we'll explore the opportunities available for our Karmic liberation from difficult people who are often related to us. Then, we'll examine the life cycle of patterns and identify ways to permanently resolve undesirable ones. Here we find a central opportunity to love ourselves in the presence of an individual who does not understand or appreciate us, and allow them to have their opinion of us and trust them with their lives.

As we know, Karma is simply cause and effect, the natural rhythm of life. However, when we have negative opinions about ourselves, others, or the causes and effects of a matter, the pattern becomes repetitive and gets stuck until we accept and make peace with ourselves and the outstanding elements and participants. As we let go of our negative evaluations, stuck Karma dissolves, and we are free to move forward in our journey. Karma is not between us and another. While other people can seem to be at the opposite end of our dynamic, they are simply stepping in to help us recognize our thoughts and feelings about our predicament. Sometimes, their behavior is dreadful; our challenge is to relinquish judgment. Let's do an exercise to better understand this Akashic Approach.

EMPOWERMENT EXERCISE #16
Resolving Current Life Difficulty

Open your Records following the Pathway Prayer protocol. Now, get settled into your Records in the compassionate company of your MTLOs. Your sense of their presence grows stronger, especially as you stop trying to see them visually. Bask in their wisdom and understanding of you.

At this time, identify a person you find difficult. This question is not for them; it is for you. You know who you have a troubling relationship with. Who is it, and what is your relationship? Are they a parent? Child? Sibling? Spouse? What is the problem? Describe the problem for you (even if they insist that there is no problem) and how you are affected by this difficulty. What happened to start this difficulty? You certainly recall when things became problematic for you. Something happened in real life. What was it? When? What was your response? What was your part in it? Check to see what decisions you made in the past that contributed to this unfortunate situation.

Certainly, other people do terrible things to us at various points in time. This person may have done something awful. How did you respond? What did you think about it? What did you think about yourself in this situation? Next, let's see if you want something from them that they don't have. Is there something they want that you cannot give?

Ask your MTLOs to help you see this person as they are seen and known in the Light of Truth and accept the reality of this relationship. What is the best that you can ever expect from this relationship? Can you accept that it may never be what you want it to be? Is it possible for you to extend kindness and respect to yourself even though this situation is so challenging, even though you cannot resolve this relationship, even though you cannot make it the way you want it to be? Is it possible for you to be your authentic self in the presence of this person? To love and appreciate yourself in their company even if this situation never changes? Are you willing to stop trying to change this person and allow them to be the way they are?

Now close your Records by reading the Closing Prayer out loud. You may want to pause to make some notes. With that, let's turn our attention to the next issue at hand.

Life Cycle of Patterns

Every pattern has its life cycle. Those patterns are always positive in their original intent and chosen as structures to support us in our lives, creating an energetic design through which energy flows both to us and away from us. Patterns serve as filters helping us to organize planetary Life based on our beliefs. Ancestral patterns are especially supportive because an entire group of people uses them. Patterns support our growth: as we develop, an old pattern that was once a great asset becomes limiting. We may not even notice a pattern of behavior until it becomes uncomfortable. This cycle is natural to all patterns. Discomfort is a sign that we have outgrown our need for this particular way of behaving.

Resistance, rejection, condemnation, and negative judgment keep patterns in place. If we have a harsh idea about ourselves for having a certain pattern or negatively assessing it, it will become stuck because negativity fosters stuckness. On the other hand, acceptance facilitates release. As we come to understand and appreciate the positive value of any pattern, it can begin to dissolve (if that is what is best for us). With judgment, they stay, and we are stuck. When we let go of our condemning attitudes, the pattern loosens and falls away—and we find ourselves in a state of greater freedom.

The Law of Authentic Identity can be helpful as we strive to avoid blaming others or ourselves. We always take on patterns that are beneficial for us. We never adopt harmful patterns; it is an energetic impossibility. What enables a pattern to stick is our emotional, mental harmony. And so we can only take on something from others that is ours, something we already believe. No one can ever force a pattern on us that we disagree with. (For example, my father wanted me to be a secretary, but that was not aligned with my beliefs about who I was.)

We only grab onto those ideas others carry that make good sense to us. Otherwise, we will not even be tempted to adopt an idea.

Similarly, we only release what no longer works for us and will not let go until we are ready. Sometimes, we think we are ready before we are actually ready. But, just like in nature, patterns fall away when they have fulfilled their purpose in supporting us, like leaves on a tree.

Since we are all interconnected, it is natural to give and receive ideas, patterns, perspectives, etc. As we take responsibility for our part in all relationships, any tendency toward victim consciousness begins to dissolve. Recognizing that we are simply swapping ideas and beliefs that fit our current level of consciousness prevents us from getting stuck in the long term with difficult ideas that will interfere with realizing our dreams.

Our next exercise is a wonderful way to begin our journey of conscious freedom from limiting ancestral patterns. As with all of our practices, consider this a beginning. Let yourself be a beginner for this segment of your spiritual quest.

EMPOWERMENT EXERCISE #17
Freedom from Limiting Patterns

Open your Records using the Pathway Prayer Process. Now, settle in with your MTLOs. With every excursion into your Records, you become increasingly familiar with the space, the atmosphere, and your response to it. Notice how comfortable you've become within the heart of your Records.

As if you are confiding in trusted friends, identify and describe a pattern of behavior you share with family members who are currently causing you difficulty. This pattern of behavior is not a secret to you; you can identify and describe it because it has become uncomfortable, and you frequently notice it. Describe your behaviors that make up this pattern. What do you do or avoid doing? What steps do you take when you are involved in it? You'll notice that it is very specific, not vague or random. Give yourself a chance to explain this to your MTLOs.

When did you first adopt this pattern? What was going on in your life that caused you to begin doing this? Remember, when you chose this way of behaving, it was very appealing. What made it seem to be such a good idea for you at the time? How did it benefit you at the time? In what ways did this behavior solve a problem you were facing? What convinced you this was a wise choice for you?

Now, ask your MTLOs to help you identify other people in your family line in this lifetime who have this pattern as well. You know who they are. What inspired them to adopt this pattern? Was it the same as your motivation? How has this pattern spread throughout your family? What did everyone expect from this pattern? How did they expect it would be beneficial for them? In what ways was it beneficial?

At what point in this life did this pattern become a problem for you? What happened? What are some possible consequences of letting go of this pattern? Will it upset your relationships with your relatives? Will it bring you closer to others?

Since it has been such a deep pattern in your family and people seem to have it for long periods of time, you may have it for the rest of your life. Are you willing to treat yourself with kindness and respect even though you have this pattern? Can you extend warmth and appreciation to yourself just the way you are right now?

Close your Records. Pause to make some notes for yourself.

Every family group has both positive and negative traits. Part of the reason you selected your family is because of their wonderful personality traits. While it is absolutely true that you are here to find freedom from the limitations of your ancestral line, it is also true that you are here to embrace and enjoy the positive qualities of this group. Let's do another exercise to clarify positive traits to consciously cultivate in ourselves.

EMPOWERMENT EXERCISE #18

Embracing Positive Ancestral Patterns

Open your Records following the protocol. Centering into your Records, establish your Pillar of Light. You know how to do this and can navigate your own Records quickly. Move into the sanctuary of your sacred space. Your Pillar of Light is set up with the simple thought that it is in place—and so it is!

Ask your MTLOs to assemble your relatives, parents, grandparents, great-grandparents, etc., going back in time a generation at a time, following the last as far back as you can imagine—all in your Pillar of Light. Next, gather your siblings, cousins, second cousins, in-laws, nieces and nephews, etc., extending out as far and wide as you can imagine. Holding all these people in the Pillar of Light, ask your MTLOs to illuminate the space so you can recognize the best traits and characteristics of this group. We seek positive personal qualities: abilities, valuable traits, and characteristics.

For the next few moments, ask to become aware of only the best aspects of your group. Identify what they are and make a note of these qualities. Ask your MTLOs to empower you to recognize how you fit into this group from this angle. Out of these shared traits, which do you have? What qualities are you carrying? What is the opportunity for you? Ask your MTLOs to help you to understand what you can do to bring the very best of these people to life in the world today. How can you do this in this lifetime? How can you honor the best of your ancestors?

Close your Records. Pause to make some notes.

EMPOWERMENT EXERCISE #19

Three-Level Reading for Ancestral Patterns

When working with others, it is very helpful to follow these steps to explore and resolve their issues. We consider the Three Levels of readings: the Story, Causes and Conditions, and Soul-Level Truth regarding Ancestral Patterns.

LEVEL ONE: THE STORY

- What happened to your client?

- What is the problem? Describe it.

- Avoid labels. Watch for your judgments about the people involved and the situation.

- Accept this as their reality at this time.

LEVEL TWO: CAUSES AND CONDITIONS

- Look for patterns of thought, beliefs, and behavior in the family line that reflect ancestral influences/specific ancestral relationships. Explore when, where, and why your client adopted the Ancestral Patterns.

- How has this served the client? Notice the valuable ways this pattern has been helpful to your client.

- What convinced your client that this was a wise strategy? Describe how it was a very smart selection.

- Notice how this behavior has been helpful to everyone in the family group.

- Make room within your heart for the reality of who they are and their heroic quest through the human journey. Your Acceptance ignites transformation. Your judgment thwarts healing.

LEVEL THREE: SOUL-LEVEL TRUTH

- What are the real benefits of this pattern for your client?

- How has this pattern empowered their awakening, growth, and development?

- Can you extend respect and compassion to your client even though they have difficulty with this pattern?

- Is it possible that, even though this pattern is a problem at this point in time, it isn't powerful enough to stop your client from being a loving human being?

- Take a moment to let yourself love this person, understand and appreciate them, and know that they are truly amazing. Even though they have had some serious challenges, you can't help but fall in love with them!

Close the Records and make some notes.

The primary purpose of selecting an ancestral line is to facilitate our awakening to our goodness and that of others. Remember that it is unnecessary and impossible to cut cords with members of our Soul Groups. We are one, and nothing we do can change that fact. Look for the positive value of the relationship and experience for your client. It is there. If you, the Practitioner, get it, so will your client. We begin our next section with an exercise designed to center you in the reality of Oneness within yourself.

EMPOWERMENT EXERCISE #20
Centering in Oneness

Open your Records using the Pathway Prayer Process. Adjust yourself into your Records and sense your MTLOs' infinite understanding and compassion for you. Bring your awareness to your heart space, in the middle of your chest, allowing yourself to settle in.

Direct your attention to your back body as if you could see out through the back of your heart space. Here you will find all the expressions of who you have been in other times and places: people you have been in all your prior incarnations, coming together to contribute to your success in this life—all lining up to love, support, and empower you in your life now.

Now, open your awareness to your left and your right. On both sides are all the expressions of who you were in other times and places when you learned to be a good, loyal, and understanding friend to yourself. Throughout your lifetimes, you've learned to connect with yourself, listen, and act on your Truth. You've discovered wonderful ways to honor and respect yourself no matter your circumstances. These are versions of you in other beautiful incarnations gathering as your most loyal friends in this life.

Now, bring your attention to your feet, resting on the Earth. Find here all the expressions of who you have been in other times and places when you brought great accomplishment and service to the world. Throughout your Soul's journey, you have had the chance to make significant contributions to improving the quality of life for many people, in numerous areas of life, on many continents, at many different times. Stand on the shoulders of your contributions throughout time.

Next, direct your awareness to the space above you. Open up to the lifetimes of recognizing and receiving Divine guidance and wisdom, the eternal connections you have made, shining your way to this life and through this life. The Light has been your constant companion no matter where your journeys happen to be—shining the way ahead, supporting you in any given moment, and following behind as you make your way in the world.

Finally, face forward to your future. Look at who you are becoming. See or sense the spiritual qualities you are cultivating: compassion, wisdom, kindness, respect, and so many others. Lifetime after lifetime, you've been releasing obstacles to your magnificence, unleashing the infinite love within, and expressing the best of who you are to the world.

Stand in the awareness of your oneness through time. In this very moment, you are one within yourself. You are one with who you have been and who you are becoming—now and always. You are one with the Divine—now and always. Your oneness is real. Enjoy it.

Close your Records, reading the Closing Prayer out loud. Pause to make your notes.

RECONCILING PAST LIVES

n this segment of our Akashic Adventure, we focus on a key to our individual unity: Reconciling Past Lives. First, let's examine some of the essential ideas supporting effective work in this area.

Always start in the present moment. Never go into a past life; there is only the present. Because we never know in advance if an issue is rooted in a past life, our focus always begins in this lifetime, with the ordinary challenges we address in the present. Ask for the origin of the problem, when it began. If it began in another time and place, that will be made clear in the Records. So, become aware of who you were in another time and place, and let this awareness come. As long as we keep an open mind about the origin of an issue, we will be led to the Truth.

In the Records, we recognize that the Eternal Soul experiences a variety of incarnations to grow into unconditional self-love and embrace its Divine nature, no matter what external evidence indicates. Each lifetime we experience is an opportunity to expand our ability to love ourselves no matter what. Often we face the challenge of loving, respecting, and appreciating ourselves after we've been extremely harsh, critical, and judgmental of ourselves for not living up to our ideals. From an Akashic point of view, the purpose of reincarnation is to give us ample opportunity to master unconditional self-love, love of others, and all of creation. It is helpful to consider your specific life within that framework to encourage optimal growth.

Past life reconciliation uses the three-level pattern for Energy Healing in readings. The MTLOs allow us to interact with who we were in other times and places to resolve problems, relinquish judgments, and access wisdom gained in prior incarnations—all supporting the process of increasing unconditional self-love. In past life work, we discover that, while others may have done horrible things to us, what disturbs and limits us throughout time are our own choices and actions. We often are upset by who we have been and what we have done or failed to do in prior times. The behavior of others may undoubtedly be awful, but our most crippling criticisms are for ourselves and our responses and lack of responses to situations we encounter. In past life work, we are challenged to love and accept who we have been in other times and places. We are presented with a significant opportunity to recognize that we are unified within ourselves. Each of us is a Soul revealed through various human expressions over time and space.

While working in the Records, Past Lives come into our awareness when we have yet to accept who we were at that time. We do not need or receive full details of the entire Incarnation. Rather, what's available to us is the general outline of who we have been, the choices we have made, and how those selections have affected us throughout our lives, but especially now. We glimpse a sliver of life at a decisive moment. Some people are visual and will "see" Past Lives; a few will "hear," but 85 percent of us will have a "felt sense"—an awareness of who we were, when, where, and why. It is perfect and all that is necessary for transforming our relationship with our experience.

Once we make peace with ourselves, the pressure or energy of the past life is released, and we are relieved. The energy we have been holding with our judgment is gone and no longer impacts us. This process sometimes results in the complete eradication of a pattern, but more often, it diminishes the intensity of the pattern, accelerating complete release. The Record is not a fishpond of Past Lives for our entertainment. Instead, Past Lives are revealed as they pertain to current life challenges.

Resolving Difficulties

What do we mean by "difficulty?" We use this term to identify our next area of growth, perhaps a stubborn problem from the past or a confusing situation in a present life circumstance. Additionally, it can be a thorny matter we are currently addressing in a project we are involved in. As humans on a Soul journey, we are always moving away from trouble and toward our dreams. In our work, we know both directions present challenges to address. You always know what is most important to you at any given time. When your questions are sincere, the Records always respond with great wisdom and compassion. Now is a good time to explore these ideas.

EMPOWERMENT EXERCISE #21
Three-Level Reading for Past Lives

Open your Records following the protocol of the Prayer. Take this opportunity to consciously reconnect with your MTLOs. Request their assistance with resolving an issue you currently face in your life—something troubling you at this time. They are always available to support you but never come forward without an invitation. They have immense respect for you and wait for you to call on them.

LEVEL ONE: THE STORY

As if you are sitting with your most trusted spiritual advisors, describe what is happening or not happening in your life right now that is causing you distress. What happened? How did you respond? What type of problem are you facing? What are the consequences or results of your decisions and actions? How are you being affected by this problem?

LEVEL TWO: CAUSES AND CONDITIONS

(NOTE: For your own past life work, use a Pillar of Light; but do *not* use a Pillar of Light with a client in a reading.)

Establish a Pillar of Light. Simply imagine that there is a Pillar of Light about an arm's distance in front of you—and there it is. Next, connect to the Pillar with a bridge of Light from your heart to the Pillar. Use this Pillar as a "viewing screen" for this exercise.

Ask your MTLOs to bring to your awareness the point of origin of your current difficulty. When did this problem begin? Get a sense or observe who you were in another time and place. Make a note of some of your general features: your gender, race, socioeconomic class, region on the planet, type of work, family, etc. Any pertinent info will be easy to identify. If you struggle to grasp the information, it is not important. All you need to know is approximately when, where, and why you made the choice causing difficulty in your life.

Do your best to describe how things seem to your MTLOs. As you describe, you will find your awareness getting stronger when you connect with the Truth and weaker if you are off the mark. Experiment with your description until you find a comfortable path of awareness. What happened then that is contributing to your difficulty now? Describe the circumstances. What occurred? How did you respond? What actions did you take, what decisions did you make that affect you today? What convinced you that this behavior was in your best interest at the time? In what ways has it been beneficial, then and even now? You always make the best possible selections. What inspired you to make this choice? What were the valid reasons for this decision? Can you understand and respect yourself for your choices in that time? Does your behavior make sense to you? If not, continue to ask for insight, guidance, and wisdom from your MTLOs.

LEVEL THREE: SOUL-LEVEL TRUTH

With the new understanding you have about yourself, consider how your choice and subsequent behavior are evidence of the profound love you have for yourself. Give yourself credit for the exceptional wisdom and kindness you exhibited at the time. Extend respect, kindness, and hospitality to who you were in another time and place.

With the support of your MTLOs, open your heart center and invite this expression of who you were into your heart space. Escort this person across the bridge of light from the Pillar into your heart space. Make room within yourself for this part of you. Notice how you feel about this person. Ask what this individual needs from you to experience safety and welcome. Do your best to honor their requests. (After 24–48 hours, this aspect of yourself will be absorbed into the greater whole of you. You will continue to increase your awareness of the unity of your being.)

Let the Pillar collapse. Close your hands over your heart center. Imagine a ribbon of Light moving from the left side of your body to the right and another from the right to the left as if you were swaddling a baby. Take a deep breath and enjoy yourself.

Close your Records following the protocol. Pause to make notes about your experience.

Accessing Wisdom of Past Lives

Many of the gifts of our growth are embedded in the fabric of our Souls. They are treasures we carry through our journey. When we need these gems, they become accessible to us. However, skills and talents are not. As you can imagine, the best skills we developed in other times are not up to present-day standards and of no practical use today. And yet, the consciousness, awareness, and approach to Life we cultivated in other times and places can be very helpful to us now. For example, if I was an engineer 1,000 years ago, my approach to problem-solving would still be useful, along with the sense of priorities developed in that lifetime. Still, the instruments and mathematical formulas would be outdated and useless in any current situation.

Keep in mind that our work is always centered in the present. When engaged in a project, we can always seek the support of who we were in other times and places to empower our success—as long as we are realistic about the usefulness of approach and consciousness. As persons unified with all our experiences over time, we can consciously connect with the perspectives that have brought us excellence and success in other lifetimes. In our next exercise, we will activate greater awareness of our unity.

EMPOWERMENT EXERCISE #22
Unity of Past Lives

Open your Records using the Pathway Prayer Process. Connect with your MTLOs and review your current project: describe what you are doing, how it is progressing, how it is easy and flowing, and the challenges you face.

Establish your Pillar of Light about an arm's distance in front of you, with a Light bridge connecting your heart to the Pillar. Ask your MTLOs to direct your attention to who you were in another time and place to assist you with this project. Get acquainted with this individual: the basics of who, when, where, and what they were doing in their lifetime. Find out what they know and how they can contribute to your success. Invite this individual into your heart space. Escort them across the bridge of Light and give them a chance to get comfortable within you. Let yourself be infused with their wisdom and point of view. Thank them in advance for their support, and ask what you can do to further your connection.

Allow the Pillar of Light to dissolve by simply taking your attention away and closing your heart space by wrapping a ribbon of Light from left to right and another from right to left.

Close the Records by reading the Closing Prayer out loud. Pause to make some notes for yourself.

Practitioner Tips

Doing this work with others is both fascinating and powerful. When a client comes for a reading, we always begin in the present, with a challenge being faced in this lifetime. We listen to the difficulty and explore the origin of the trouble. If the problem began in a previous life, that will become abundantly clear.

When accessing Past Lives for a client, the awareness and transformation of the situation occur through the Practitioner, not the client. It is your responsibility as Practitioner to become aware of the significant Incarnation, the decisions made, and the subsequent impact of the choices. Because the Practitioner has temporary authority over the client's grid (provided when the client permitted the Practitioner to open the Records), it is the Practitioner's job to move through the Three Levels of the Reading and describe the experience for the client. Having progressed through the levels for yourself, you can then do this on behalf of your client.

The client will not have awareness of the past life but will resonate with the Truth as you speak it. As the Practitioner "falls in love" with the client, outstanding judgments fall away, and the client experiences kindness, respect, and understanding—igniting their healing process and growth into unconditional self-love. As Practitioner, check yourself for any judgments, negative reactions, or opinions. Know yourself and ask for help in the Records as you move through the levels. The acceptance, kindness, respect, and understanding of the Practitioner make all the difference—and actually activate an adjustment in the client's grid. Watch to see if you are trying to force an idea on your client or insist that they get it. This approach will interfere with the client's shift.

As Akashic Practitioners, we develop a powerful awareness of our Oneness with our clients. This awareness can result in exceptional results for the people we serve. We know that our consciousness determines the success of a reading. We are the ones that can bring great healing and relief to others through the clarity of our awareness. Understand from the Akashic perspective that *We are One* and that the Practitioner is 100 percent responsible for the shift. As we adjust to the idea that we are one with our clients and that they are an expression of the one Life we all share, and even a representation of who we are (or have been in another time and place), we begin to love and accept them "as is." This is the power of healing. As we embrace this spiritual Truth, they are transformed. The consciousness of Oneness is profound.

WORKING WITH OTHERS

Inner & Outer Aspects

Now that you have a strong and flexible foundation, let's continue our exploration. In this segment, we will be learning about building and sustaining a successful practice of working in the Records for yourself and others. While we have been strengthening our skills to bring our spiritual gifts to the world, we now turn our attention to our own relationship to the Records and the elements of a powerful practice.

There are both inner and outer aspects of practice when working with others. Let's take a closer look at how our human condition impacts our ability to transmit and serve. There is no question that your well-being affects your ability to be effective with others. We strive for spiritual fitness to successfully serve others with insight, guidance, and wisdom from the Akasha. Our interpretation of spiritual fitness and beliefs about the Records have a significant impact on our use of this resource and our expectations for ourselves and our clients. It is very helpful to understand our needs and how we meet them as we bring Akashic Light into the world.

Inner Aspects: Awareness & Acceptance

When we talk about spiritual fitness, we refer to the condition of humility. Humility is the awareness of the limitations and imperfections of being human and the magnitude of our Soul, which is unlimited, eternal, and immortal all at the same time. As we recognize that we are incorruptible Souls on a human journey, we grow into unconditional self-love. Spiritual fitness recognizes Infinite Light shining through our finite human selves and has no negative judgment about it.

The healing paradox embedded in the second Stanza of the Pathway Prayer Process directs us to take attention off ourselves and turn our thoughts to others and how we can help them—which may seem impossible when we are in turmoil or not feeling well. Yet, it is entirely possible to be "a work in progress" with issues and incompletions in our own lives and still do a wonderful job assisting other people's transformations. This calls for us to be clear about our strengths, needs, and limitations. We must know how to care for ourselves as we make our way through life so that we can comfortably step into our place as spiritual Lightworkers in the world. The challenge is taking good enough care of ourselves to be sufficiently fit to extend ourselves to others.

The work we do with ourselves and others in the Records is in the family of spiritual counseling for personal growth, transformation, insight, and understanding. Akashic Records work is not a substitute for medical attention, professional support (legal, accounting, media, etc.), or psychological intervention. This can be confusing, especially when the Records may offer beneficial support for these issues. When you need a lawyer, get one. If it's a medical doctor, then find one. Whether we seek an accountant, real estate professional, car mechanic, or another assistant, the world is full of well-trained people who can bring specific skills to meet the difficulties we encounter in everyday life.

And even though the Records are based on sound psychological ideas, this work is not a substitute for, nor is it intended to replace good psychological help. I have found it helpful to ask my MTLOs for support in locating the best possible professional for my situation, asking for strength and courage to find the best person. Remember that the Records are not a shortcut to successful living! They are a spiritual resource providing the insight, guidance, and wisdom needed to make the best possible use of our human faculties.

Consider every segment of your Akashic practice as a mirror of your present consciousness (always growing and improving) and a demonstration of the Absolute Truth that "We are all one." As humans, our needs reside in a few categories: physical, emotional, mental, and spiritual health. Although everyone requires food, clothing, and shelter, we all have different needs in each area. Some require luxury items; others are minimalists. Some of us are carnivores; others are vegetarian. All expressions are valid. Many seek intimate life partners; others prefer a solitary life. Some thirst for career expression and fulfillment, while others hunger for artistic satisfaction. We make no judgment about any area of life or whether a person has strong drives or none at all. As Souls on the human journey, each of us will have the chance to experience options. It is all part of the process empowering us to expand our ability to know and love ourselves—no matter what!

Let's open our Records to begin examining our human selves with spiritual Light.

EMPOWERMENT EXERCISE #23
Self-Acceptance

Open your Records following the Pathway Prayer protocol we've been using all along. Settle in with your MTLOs. Sense their presence and undivided attention for you. Bathe in the acceptance and appreciation they have for you. It is precious to be aware of these qualities, especially since you never see them, only sense them. Allow yourself to be saturated with these attributes of love here in the heart of your own Akashic Records.

Now, let them know of your deep desire to bring Light and love to the world through the Akashic Records, using the Pathway Prayer Process. Share as you would with trusted friends or advisors. Request their guidance and direction in this venture. In partnership with them, consider these questions.

- What personal needs of mine require greater attention so I can be more available to my clients?

- Does my body need renewed attention from me? Is my emotional health sound? Are my thoughts clear and generally optimistic? Or do I tend toward negative confusion?

- Am I actively trusting in the goodness of Life, a loving power and presence that's part of me and still greater than I am?

- As a steward for myself, who is responsible for my care and well-being? Notice whether I have the basics in order: food, clothing, shelter, work, money, creativity. Are all of these in harmony with my requirements for satisfaction at this point in my life? Do they accurately represent who I am in the world? Or am I ready for a chance to update my relationship with Life?

- How can I support myself in having these needs met? Is there something I need to know or understand before making any changes?

- What practical actions do you suggest? How can I take care of myself in these ways without causing unnecessary stress on myself or those I love?

(Humility and healthy self-acceptance are essential for our growth. We cannot move from where we are until we make peace with who we are, the choices we've made, and the actions we've taken so far. When we arrive at self-acceptance, the process of releasing limited ideas, patterns, and even people begins—often resulting in dramatic changes greater than anything we could engineer on our own.)

Ask your MTLOs to help identify areas of strong and weak self-acceptance. Make a note of what they are. Get a sense of your patterns: what makes it easy for you to be self-accepting? What makes it difficult? Try not to be critical; just observe and be kind to yourself.

What practical suggestions do your MTLOs have to remedy this situation? Is there something for you to know or understand so you can expand your arena of self-acceptance? Are there particular actions you need to take to move forward?

Take a moment to let the Gratitude in your heart bubble up and flow out into your Records. You are a naturally gracious person, and Life appreciates that quality in you. Enjoy it.

Now is the time to close the Records, done simply by reading the Closing Prayer. Go ahead and pause so you can make some notes.

Inner Aspects of Your Practice

Let's turn our attention to the inner aspects of our practice. By inner aspects, I mean self-awareness and your relationship with the Records. We've been cultivating certain attributes of love throughout lifetimes, developing our inherent abilities to respect, honor, appreciate, and understand ourselves and others. This tiny sample of qualities is just the beginning of the internal treasures embedded in your Soul which are being brought to the surface as you grow and become the person you are meant to be.

In the next exercise, we explore the relationship between our experiences and the characteristics strengthening our service to others.

EMPOWERMENT EXERCISE #24
Discovering Inner Aspects of Your Practice

Open your Records. Adjust yourself to the infinite wisdom of your MTLOs. (This is not cold, emotionally remote wisdom. Instead, it is warm, kind, supportive, and appreciative of us personally—as well as all human beings involved in the heroic quest to awaken awareness. The more you sense these qualities emanating from the MTLOs, the more comfortable you will feel in their presence. It is helpful to focus on their characteristics, making it easier to relax and trust them.)

Open up to the inspired partnership you have with your most trusted spiritual advisors and ask:

- Can I get a sense of the best ways to prepare myself to do readings? How can I develop my skills to be effective with them? Are there things I could do to make it easier to relax and trust the process?

- What particular interpersonal skills do I have that will help in this situation? Are there some things I need to do to improve some of my skills?

- How is my sensitivity helpful? How can I maintain my sensitivity to others while cultivating my sensitivity to the Records?

- Who am I best suited to assist? Is there a particular area of human difficulty that I can help resolve for clients? Is there a category of people I can be especially helpful to?

- What life experiences have I had that contribute to my usefulness to others? What problems do I understand? What human traits and characteristics do I have that are beneficial when working with others?

- Please help me understand the Records' perspective and how the MTLOs see me as a partner. From the point of view of the Records, what is the highest possibility for me as a Practitioner working with others? What do I need to do to manifest this possibility?

Close your Records, reading the Closing Prayer out loud. Pause so you can make some notes.

A Business Meeting with your MTLOs

The prospect of having a sit-down meeting with our MTLOs is enticing. Many of us wish for that to happen in our everyday lives to gain their perspective on issues we face on an ongoing basis. Our next exercise gives us a sense of how that might occur. Let's have a "business meeting" with our MTLOs—to explore our practice and learn how they can be helpful as we go forward—as a writing exercise. A business meeting is not a replacement for any professional assistance you need to set up your practice. (As previously mentioned, if you need a lawyer or accountant, be sure to hire one.) Instead, this is an opportunity to connect with the insight, guidance, and wisdom of the Akasha to develop your practice of working with others. Make sure you have something to write with as we go along, since this is a writing exercise.

EMPOWERMENT EXERCISE #25

A Business Meeting with Your MTLOs

Open your notebook and your Records. Get acclimated into your Records, adjusting to the peace, quiet, and support. Notice if you have a sense of the presence of your MTLOs. Whether you feel them close or sense that they are farther away, just observe your connection and how it is expressed at this time. Begin by inviting your MTLOs to a business meeting geared explicitly toward your Akashic Records practice. Let them know that there are many items on the agenda today: workspace, time, money, recordings, advertising, and even a mission statement. Let's take this one at a time:

SPACE

- What elements are essential when choosing and setting up a space to work? (There are some nonnegotiable items, such as privacy, quiet, and comfort, but the details vary with each one of us.)

- Is it better for you to have a private space, or can you share a workspace with others? Do you need it full time or part time? Is it a health or spiritual studio, or a more business-like environment?

- Can you work from home? If so, what will your clients need? Do you need parking? (We always want to make our clients as comfortable as possible and reduce stress for them in any way we can. You want your workspace to support you and your clients, so you feel safe and free to express yourself.)

- Is there a preferred location for you at this point in your business?

- Do your MTLOs have suggestions about what will support you in being fully available to your clients?

TIME

- At this point in your skill development, what is the optimal length of time for a reading: 30, 45, or 60 minutes? (It is always better to offer 30 powerful minutes than 60 tepid minutes. Use a timer to keep track of time, which gets lost when working in the Records.)

- Is there a time of day that is best for you to offer readings—morning, afternoon, or evening?

- How many days a week? Which days?

- How many readings per day? How much of a break do you need in between readings?

MONEY

- What is the appropriate amount to charge per reading at this stage of your service to others? (You are never required to charge money for readings, and as you are guided to work with others on a professional basis, you can certainly charge money for readings. The amount of money you charge must be comfortable for you, or you will unwittingly push clients away. Better to start low and build than to overcharge and not work. You can always raise your rates. Be mindful of the standard rates in your area. If you overprice or underprice, you will thwart your efforts to serve.)

- How shall I collect fees? (Pay attention to the way people in your area exchange money. Some do it electronically, others with plastic, and some even use cash. Make sure you are prepared to collect funds in a way that is convenient for your customers.)

RECORDINGS

- Will you be offering recordings? (You are welcome to record the sessions and to transfer those recordings to the client. Another option is to have the client record the session. This is especially helpful because then you are not involved in the recording and have no liability for the success or failure of the recording of the session.)

ADVERTISING

- How can you make it easy for potential clients to find you?

- What do others need to know about you and the work you do?

- What do you need to share about yourself so they know you can help them?

- Do your MTLOs have any suggestions or recommendations about your advertising? (On social media, you mustn't discuss readings you've done or clients you've seen, or even share great successes. Remember the Guideline about confidentiality—this is when it becomes critical. Do not make false promises! You will hurt too many people. Always under-promise in your advertising and overdeliver in your practice! In your advertising, when presenting your work, you can certainly say you read the Akashic Records, the archive of the Soul and its journey as human. But there is never any reason to insist that your clients know the Records! The reading is about the person, not about the Records.)

MISSION STATEMENT

- In partnership with your MTLOs, write down a two- or three-sentence statement identifying the focus and intention of your work as a Pathway Prayer Process Akashic Records Practitioner at this time. What is your purpose, what are your goals as a Practitioner?

After all of this, ask: What is the next action step to take in the upcoming week?

Close your Records by reading the Closing Prayer. Pause to review your work when your Records are closed. What do you see? How will you structure your offerings based on these insights?

Building Your Practice

You are doing intimate, spiritual work. Building a practice to serve others comes from the Soul, supported by your MTLOs. Every day, ask in your Records, "Who can I help today? How can I help?" Look for people who are struggling and offer your assistance. Let people know that you will do your very best to help them. You will look at who they are as a person and the challenges they face through the lens of the Soul. Don't concern yourself with whether they understand the Records. What's important is that you offer your assistance and provide it when called. Do not make false promises. If they say, "No," accept that as the best answer for them at this time.

We have been exploring new levels of depth in our foundation work, discovering rich possibilities for our own lives and some sacred treasures of consciousness. Let's begin with a practice in our Records designed to strengthen our connection with ourselves and the Records.

EMPOWERMENT EXERCISE #26
Empowering Spiritual Fitness

Open your Records using the Pathway Prayer Process. Take a moment to settle into the central zone of your Records, your heart in harmony with the Heart of the Records. Get a sense of the presence of your MTLOs, always available to support you but never intrusive or invasive.

Now, expand your awareness—mind, body, and Soul—and direct your attention to your physical presence on the planet, right here, right now. You are a real human being in a particular location, living in a precise time, walking through the world on a specific day. Placing all of your attention on yourself, you may notice that you occupy a particular place, a space in time that you share with no one else. You are a unique spiritual being residing in your human body, thinking with a certain mind, feeling through your emotions. Every aspect of you is valuable and deliberate.

There is not now, nor has there ever been, nor will there ever be, another person just like you. I invite you to stand in this beautiful, powerful Truth. You are a unique individual who has come to this place and time as the perfect person to experience your life and develop into the most loving person possible. Throughout this life, you may have experienced traumas and hardships. You may not have behaved in the kindest and most generous ways. Yet who you are is perfect, whole, and complete at the level of your Soul. No matter what fears or limiting beliefs you hold, you are the ideal person to express your Soul in this life. Take your rightful place—here, now.

Let yourself fully occupy this place and moment in time. As you do, the Light of Life that is the core of your being proudly shines itself through you. No matter what has happened to you, no matter what you have done or failed to do, Life is deeply pleased with you.

Close your Records. Pause and make some notes if you like.

A Note About Personal Healing

In this advanced Level II, we devote extensive attention to our healing through the Records. This is for two reasons. First, to be effective with others, we must have experience of our own personal growth and transformation using the Records. This prepares us to be clear channels for Light. We understand how the protocols work and how to guide others as we shepherd them through their processes. One of the essential laws of the Universe is that you can only transmit what you have (and you will always transmit what you have or who you are). So, for this reason, we do deep, substantial work with ourselves as preparation for our practice of working with others—and for our Soul-level satisfaction!

Sacred Wounds

This can be a baffling idea, raising many questions. How can our wounds be sacred or anything other than a problem in our relationship with ourselves? Let's look deeper into the Akashic perspective on this matter. From an Akashic point of view, we recognize that all humans throughout time experience wounds and injuries, without exception. For some reason, when Souls come to Earth, they experience various injuries. There must be a valid spiritual reason for this occurrence. While it may not be a certainty for our future lives, it has been predictable in our past. But we know that all of Life is somehow supporting our growth, so let's keep an open mind to grasp the good reasons we have these wounds and injuries.

The shift we seek is from ordinary to sacred. According to our old ideas, wounds are evidence of our unworthiness, proof of a lack of enlightenment. In days past, we might have perceived injured persons as sinners, condemned by the gods. It is time for us to embrace a new idea in this New Age. Our wounds are opportunities to connect with the Divine within and experience unconditional self-love. These injuries are simply proof of our need and heartfelt desire to grow closer to our true selves, to learn to love ourselves unconditionally, and then to allow ourselves to encounter the presence of the Ultimate Reality, God.

This new point of view opens the way to a profound, turbo-charged healing question for accelerating our growth and transformation. In light of any wounds or injuries, we ask ourselves this simple question: "Is it possible for me to love and respect myself even though I have... (fill in the blank)?" With ourselves, we ask: "How do I love and respect myself even though I have suffered/been a victim?" With others, we ask: "How can I love and respect my client/this person even though they have suffered/been a victim?" These new questions demonstrate the Akashic Approach in action—and open the way to new solutions to our ancient issues.

Akashic Approach

We all desire deep, lasting healing from the painful episodes of our lives. The Records grant great insight into this challenge and offer some deceptively simple but powerful strategies for our freedom and growth. Permanent healing requires that both inner and outer aspects harmonize. Awareness and Acceptance are inner aspects; Appropriate Action is an outer aspect. Honoring our Soul's choice to be who we are is both an inner and outer aspect. While any one of these is beneficial, both inner and outer aspects are required for lasting change. We can achieve transformation resulting in personal peace and freedom with this four-step protocol:

1 Awareness of self/awakening to self
2 Acceptance
3 Appropriate Action
4 Honoring our Soul's choice to be who we are!

Principles supporting our Akashic Approach are consistent as we move into greater depth in our practice. A simple review will help us keep the important ideas front and center in our minds. Without exception, all people are essentially, immutably good at our core. Central to the identity of every person in existence is the love at the core of their being that cannot be mutilated, destroyed, or extinguished. Even if individuals behave terribly, harming themselves or others, the goodness remains. All of Life is a Divine orchestration awakening us to this Truth. Everything, including difficulties, supports us in our cosmic quest to recognize the Truth of our goodness and that of everyone else.

Every behavior and strategy we adopt is wise and optimal at its inception. We only and always select our best option. No person ever chooses an option that is not their number one choice. And every choice we make is a deliberate selection in the hopes that it will increase love and well-being for us. Even when the action we select causes harm, we choose it in the hopes that it will increase our peace of mind and well-being.

What's more: our Souls are perfect, magnificent. There is nothing we could ever do to put out the Light of our Soul. And there is nothing anyone can do to us that would extinguish that Light. And so, naturally, there is never any need to heal the Soul. Your Soul, any person's Soul, never needs healing. The Soul cannot be anything less than perfect. A human being can be bruised and suffering, but the Soul is unscathed by difficulty.

Our first step is Awareness. This is the Awakening phase of the healing process. In times of injury of any variety, we attempt to protect ourselves by "falling asleep" to ourselves. This creates a situation of self-abandonment—the king of all wounds. Everything stems from self-abandonment, including self-neglect, self-abuse, denying, and minimizing ourselves. As long as we are in a state of self-abandonment, others must abandon us. Once we cease self-abandonment, others will no longer abandon us; they will not be able to. Others can only and always treat us the way we treat ourselves. As we awaken and become aware of our Innermost Self—treating ourselves with the respect and understanding we deserve—others will follow suit.

The Innermost Self is that facet of our inner being that knows the Truth about who we are, the dreams and hopes we have for this life, and the difficulties we have faced—but holds no judgment against us, only compassion, mercy, patience, and understanding. Let's do an exercise in the Records to stimulate awakening awareness.

EMPOWERMENT EXERCISE #27
Your Innermost Self

Open your Records using the Pathway Prayer Process. Settle into the compassionate, safe space of the Records with your MTLOs.

Consider how you habitually ignore, deny, minimize, reject, cancel, or silence yourself in everyday life. These are personal memories and will be easy to recall. You will likely notice a particular pattern you have developed using some of these more than others—that is normal. Get a sense of your standard behavior in this area. Ask your MTLOs to help you identify when this pattern began in your lifetime. What happened? What was going on? Why did you think it was such a good idea? Where did you get this idea? What convinced you it was wise to respond to yourself in this way? How has this strategy been helpful for you?

We know that the only reason you adopted this pattern of behavior is that it was so helpful at the time. Get a sense of how pushing yourself away has been wise, protecting and safeguarding some of your inner treasures. It is even possible that you will become aware of some of the precious inner gifts you have been protecting. Do not worry if you do not, but be open to this additional awareness and welcome it if it happens.

Let's focus on a specific incident. In the company of your most trusted advisors, your MTLOs, bring to mind a life situation that took you totally by surprise, one where you had no idea this situation was brewing. Or when things turned out to be far worse than you imagined. It may have seemed benign at the moment, but as time passed, the consequences were severe.

Describe what happened as you remember it. How did you respond? In the Records, spiritual healing is specific. Do your best to avoid being vague for actual events that occurred. Instead, describe what happened to the best of your ability. What occurred, and what was your response? What were you thinking? What were you feeling? What actions did you take?

Now, ask your MTLOs for support reaching out to your Innermost Self. Do your best to connect with that part of yourself you have denied for so long—this is a great opportunity to express any regret or sorrow for having neglected this precious part of yourself. It is also an opportunity to acknowledge yourself for the creative ways you've tried to love and care for yourself in difficult circumstances. Indeed, you were in a difficult situation, and your strategy for self-care was admirable.

Close your Records. Pause and make some notes.

Acceptance

Now we turn our attention to a ridiculously simple and extraordinarily profound idea: Acceptance. Acceptance is recognizing the reality of a situation and our part in it. It does not require approval. Acceptance means that there may be events or conditions we do not like or prefer, yet we are clear that they occur or have happened in the past. An example of this is the reality of my parents' deaths. I do not like that they are gone; there are times I would love to visit with them. But that will not happen because they are deceased. I have the opportunity to accept reality even though it makes me uncomfortable. Surely you have many examples of similar situations in your life and understand what acceptance is all about.

Practicing acceptance is an effective way to grow into unconditional self-love, the ultimate spiritual practice. Remember that a spiritual practice is any activity supporting our awareness of the Divine, training us to know and love ourselves as we are known and loved by Life itself. Energetically, acceptance ignites the release of stuck patterns of behavior. Self-condemnation and rejection keep us stuck. Insisting we be hard on ourselves or unforgiving will keep us repeating behavior we honestly want to stop. Only through acceptance do we grow.

Our lack of self-acceptance occurs through many different habits. When we hold grudges, insist on unattainable standards of perfection, and nurse grievances against ourselves, we remain stuck in a cycle of painful patterns. Grievances are simply complaints against ourselves for things we have done or failed to do. They may be justified, but they are never helpful in the long run. We do not deny our mistakes or pretend they do not exist. Instead, we recognize, identify, apologize if necessary, and then let go. After we have properly addressed our error, we turn toward positive action and get on with life.

Get on your side no matter what you have done or failed to do. Find a way to align with yourself, even if you are not pleased with your behavior. Stretch to understand your reasoning. Say to yourself in all situations, "I am here. You cannot scare me away. It's okay. No wonder you did that. Of course." Align with your Innermost Self.

One of the laws of the Universe is that other people can give us only what we give ourselves. We can only receive from others what we receive from ourselves. We may want another to be nice, forgiving, and nonjudgmental with us. However, it is energetically impossible for this to happen until we head in the direction of self-acceptance. We must offer those treasures of kindness to ourselves the best way we know how. When we do, others are free to give us more of what we desire.

The ultimate question is, "How do I love and respect myself even though I have this challenge?" This is our turbo-charged healing question. Remember, everything works together to awaken us to our Soul's perfection. Let's do an exercise to experience this practice.

EMPOWERMENT EXERCISE #28
Acceptance

Open your Records using the Pathway Prayer Process. Relax into the sanctuary of infinite kindness, respect, and understanding that is your Akashic Records. Open up to the presence of your protective, generous MTLOs, whom you can sense even though you never see them visually. This is an atmosphere of clarity and wisdom; you are completely safe in this space.

Bring to mind a grievance or complaint you have against yourself. Identify an issue or problem in your life. Something you are doing or not doing that makes you upset with yourself. Be as specific as possible. Describe the behavior to yourself. What do you do or fail to do? What happens? Why are you so upset with yourself? What about this behavior is so upsetting to you? Describe the details of what you have done or failed to do. Review the reasons causing you distress.

Keeping your focus on this Incarnation, when in this lifetime did the problem start? What were the ordinary human causes? What happened? We know you only initiated this behavior because it was helpful. What was going on in your life? What problem were you solving with this behavior?

Are you aware of other options? You always make the best possible choice even when the menu of solutions is not great. Can you see that this was the best idea you had at the time? What was so compelling about this behavior that convinced you to adopt it?

Do your best to understand what you did and why you did it. Be compassionate with yourself. You love yourself and always have. The choice you made was your attempt to find love, safety, and well-being in a challenging situation.

Say, "Of course that is the way you would respond. No wonder; it's okay. I'm here with you anyway." (Experiment with phrases that trigger a feeling of being all right in difficult situations. The sentiment of acceptance and understanding for yourself is more important than the exact words.)

Now consider how this behavior has been beneficial for you. You may be very clear about how it was helpful when you first implemented it. Go ahead and reflect on how this has been beneficial over your life. Let yourself become aware of the valid reasons for your choice. Stretch your thinking to understand what convinced you that this was a wise approach. If you have difficulty getting to a place of acceptance, ask your MTLOs to help you.

You may have this difficulty, this trait, for the rest of this life. Maybe you will change, and maybe you will not. Are you still willing to treat yourself with respect and dignity? Is it possible for you to participate in life and contribute your gifts, talents, and abilities even though you have this imperfection? Again, extend kindness, respect, and understanding to yourself. If necessary, ask your MTLOs to help you.

Close your Records following the protocol. Pause to make notes.

Having examined the inner aspects of permanent healing—awareness and acceptance—we will explore the outer aspect of Appropriate Action and the combination inner/outer aspect of honoring our Soul's choice to be who we are.

Outer Aspects: Appropriate Action & the Inner Triangle

Now we turn our attention to the outer aspects of healing: Appropriate Action and its support partner, the Inner Triangle, composed of Heart, Mind, and Will. From there, we will delve into the Zone of Choice to discover the valid reasons our Souls selected us, as people, for this lifetime.

We know the Earth plane is an arena of action, where events rooted in our consciousness—including our thoughts and feelings—come to pass physically and materially. I like to think of life on Earth as the physical expression of the internal activity of all humans throughout time. Becoming increasingly aware of our Innermost Self and cultivating the spiritual practice of unconditional self-love and acceptance provides tremendous relief—and there's more! Our next step is to act on the deep Truth of our Innermost Self to experience and express our treasured authenticity. The spiritual life is not a theory; it must be lived. While it is gratifying to meditate, reflect, and discuss spiritual ideas, putting them into practice initiates desired changes.

When considering making a move on our own behalf, we first distinguish between Appropriate and Inappropriate Action. Differences between the two are important and will determine our satisfaction. Inappropriate Action is characterized by inconsistencies in our abilities to love and care for ourselves and those we love. While we may harmoniously advocate for, provide for, and protect ourselves and others, we often fail and cause turmoil for everyone involved, bringing about results opposing our true needs.

Appropriate action is characterized by consistently providing for, advocating for, and protecting ourselves and those we love. Taking action invites us to expand our trust in Life and ourselves so we can keep an open mind and heart. Dictating the terms of our actions or insisting on specific outcomes indicates our level of fear. Openness to new outcomes and possibilities suggests a positive trust in Life and ultimately delivers us to our highest good.

In this process, we frequently affirm our thoughts, responses, and choices as we understand them by saying something like, "Of course, that's what you said/did/felt. It was a good idea at the time." The next step is to ask, "How can I help you?" and stay open to the next right step. You may wonder, "How will I know if it's the right thing to do?" Simple: you will be able to do it. If you are inspired to move in the direction of an action that is impossible for you at this time, then that's the signal that it's not your best option. The Records never encourage us to harm ourselves, spend money we don't have, ingest substances that hurt us, or be rude and disrespectful to anyone, including ourselves. Remember that the spiritual path is one of love, so all decisions emanating from this path are loving. Let's do an exercise to explore applying these ideas.

EMPOWERMENT EXERCISE #29
Appropriate Action

Open your Records using the Prayer. Settle into your Records in the loving company of your MTLOs, noticing how it feels for you to be accepted, understood, and supported. Now, take a moment to set up your personal Pillar of Light, about an arm's distance in front of you. All you have to do is think of it, and it is done. Use the Pillar as a viewing station or screen to see or sense the presence of past experiences.

Throughout your lifetimes, you have had many experiences expressing your deepest Truth through action. Sometimes they were appropriate and, at other times, inappropriate. Ask your MTLOs to show you or give you a sense of the many lifetimes you've lived in which you had great difficulty taking Appropriate Action, no matter the reason. Now, ask them to give you a glimpse of one lifetime in particular in which you had a tough time aligning your actions with your inner Truth. In a general way, who were you: what was your gender, race, and occupation? Approximately when was this? You don't need a specific date, just a general sense of the timeframe. Where were you? Again, you don't need the actual location, just the pertinent information such as the type of environment (farm, city, island, mountain, etc.) and the nature of your challenge. What quality in your character made it so hard for you? What did you find difficult about taking actions that expressed your Truth? Can you sense that you were doing your utmost to take care of yourself? Perhaps you were confused about many things, but your dedication to yourself was evident. Is it possible for you to extend kindness and respect to who you were in that time and place? Let this go simply by taking your attention away.

Ask your MTLOs to help you recognize many lifetimes in which you had a very good relationship with Appropriate Action. There are scores of experiences where it was completely easy and natural for you. Now, ask for a glimpse of awareness of one lifetime in particular when you had a clear connection between your inner Truth and outer expression. What made it so easy for you to do this? What qualities in your character made this possible? Extend Gratitude to yourself for your successes and all the growth and wisdom you have earned throughout time. Let this go simply by taking your attention away.

Bring your awareness to yourself in this lifetime, to a troubling current life situation that directly results from a problem you have with Appropriate Action. What is the problem? Specifically describe your behavior, noting what you do or avoid doing that causes the difficulty. At some point, something convinced you that this was a wise solution to a problem you were facing. You would never consciously take an action that caused trouble; your original intention was positive. What was it that convinced you to make this choice? And in what ways has it been helpful? Let's review the protocol: You know yourself and the problem at hand. You accept that it was your best idea at the time. You say to yourself, "Of course, if there had been a better solution, I would have picked it." Awareness and acceptance are vital but incomplete; we need to know what to do next. Reach deep into your Innermost Self and ask: "What can I do for you? How can I help?" Be open to any answer or outcome.

Ask your MTLOs to assist you in becoming more aware of what could be the next right step. What one action could you take that would honor the deepest desire of your Innermost Self? If it is overwhelming, ask for a streamlined version. The Records know we are human and do not encourage us to act beyond our present ability.

Close your Records, reading the Closing Prayer out loud. Now pause so you can make some notes.

The Inner Triangle

In making conscious choices, we use as many inner resources as possible. When exploring Appropriate Action, we call upon our Inner Triangle (Heart, Mind, and Will) to help us determine the viability of choice. Within the scope of history, we see the Triangle expressed through the following world teachers and ideas:

- The **Mind** was identified by the Buddha in approximately 500 BCE. Along with this recognition, he clarified Karma (the natural cycle of cause and effect). At that time in the evolution of human consciousness, it was understood that this cycle was infinite and that humans could do nothing to transcend undesirable patterns.

- When Jesus Christ introduced the principle of unconditional love at the beginning of the Common Era, he identified the **Heart** and the liberating principle of Love as the solution to the problem of Karma.

- Now, we are in the Age of Awakening Awareness, with each Soul becoming aware of its infinite nature, connection with all others, and the Divine. This is the **Age of the Will**, which happens not through one world teacher but through each of us. Our conscious actions can and do express our Soul.

These three elements—Mind, Heart, and Will—are alive, well, and related within each of us. This inner tripod gives us the stability that facilitates our ability to accommodate more Light and shine! It is a spiritual paradox that our effectiveness as transmitters of Light is based on the strength of these inner components of our human psyche. Increased harmony within our Inner Triangle activates our ability to accommodate more Light. Naturally, Light is equally radiant and magnetic. As we strive for balance in our Triangle, we naturally radiate more Light into life and magnetize everything we need to bring our Soul's Purposes to life.

In the West, in the second half of the 20th century, we awakened to the Mind/Heart connection. After 2012, awareness of the Will as a critical component in this paradigm has flooded the consciousness of the human family. Will is that part of us designed for manifesting, demonstrating, and making our conscious intentions real in the material world in which we live. I like to think of the Will as the avenue through which the Soul connects with earthly life and our inner values take form. Will is the point of interface or impact where the Soul's Purposes take form on Earth. Balanced Will delivers the greatest fulfillment while empowering harmony with everything it encounters. When balanced, the Will is reasonable, informed by the Mind. It is also sensitive to the self and others, embraced by the Heart. An overdeveloped Will results in force, and an underdeveloped Will results in inertia or even laziness. We all have a combination of overdeveloped and underdeveloped Will. Our opportunity is to recognize and understand our relationship with our Will so we can continue to grow and develop.

Appropriate action must meet the Inner Triangle Test. When you have an idea that you consider your next best action, take it to your Inner Triangle and ask these three questions:

- **Mind**: Does this idea make sense to me? (If it doesn't make good sense, you'll never do it. Therefore, it must be a common-sense idea for you personally.)

- **Heart**: Does it make me happy to consider this action? (The idea here is to be happy in the process, not to suffer with the hope of a possible happy ending. We cannot suffer our way into happiness.) The question is this: Does the very thought of this action make me happy?

- **Will**: Am I willing to take this action? Does this motivate me to take action?

Now let's do an exercise to practice applying the Triangle Test to any situation.

EMPOWERMENT EXERCISE #30

The Inner Triangle Test

Open your Records using the Pathway Prayer Process. Get comfortable in your Records, in the presence of your MTLOs.

Whatever action you are considering, achieving fulfillment requires that your idea meet the Inner Triangle Test. The action must have the approval and enthusiasm of your Mind, Heart, and Will.

- Bring to **Mind** an action you've been considering, something you have been thinking about doing in your life. It could be any ordinary human action, from something simple like baking a cake to something more complex such as moving to another country. The action needs to be real and measurable, discernible to the human eye. Take this idea and bring it into your mind. What do you think of it? Does it make sense to you? Is it a "good idea" for you at this time? Or does this idea seem a little unreasonable?

- Now, bring this idea to your **Heart**. How do you feel about this idea? Does it make you happy and excited? Does it give you pleasure to ponder it? Or does it fill you with anxiety and dread?

- Next, go to your **Will**. Bring your idea to your Will. When contemplating this potential action, are you inspired to act? Or not? Does the very thought of this idea stimulate you to act? Or to hide?

Now close your Records and pause to make some notes.

Our Soul's Choice

Ultimately, our transformation comes to life as we honor our Soul's choice to be who we are! It is an exclusive, sacred opportunity to honor that who we are as people is our Soul's first and best choice. Who we are as people and the lives we live are no accident, but an optimal selection.

For our next exploration in the Records, we engage in the Zone of Choice. As previously mentioned, this is a realm within the Records that we visit between lifetimes to decide the particulars that will support the next stage of our development. It is an exciting realm with infinite possibilities that come into focus as we evolve. Additionally, it can be very intense and highly charged. To work in the Zone of Choice, make this excursion only with your MTLOs. (Reminder: Never lead a client into this realm: it is never necessary and can actually be counterproductive.) This realm is for you because of your advancing consciousness readying you for greater clarity and depth.

EMPOWERMENT EXERCISE #31
The Zone of Choice

Open your Records using the Pathway Prayer Process. Give yourself the chance to settle into your Records in the loving company of your MTLOs.

Ask your MTLOs to help you get to the place known as the Zone of Choice. You can travel by moving up and out, beyond the self, or down and into the self. Any one of these options is perfect. As you arrive, ask your MTLOs to help you get some clarity on the intentions and purposes of your Soul in this Incarnation. What were some of your Soul's aspirations, goals, objectives, and intentions for this specific Incarnation? All things considered, including this time in history and your individual identity, what were your hopes?

Ask your MTLOs to return you to that place in time and space when your Soul took a stand, considered every option on Earth, looked for the ideal vehicle through which it would realize its Destiny, and chose you! What was so compelling about the person you are that your Soul found so irresistible? Recognize that you are the perfect person to demonstrate your Soul's Purposes in this Incarnation. What details of you and your ordinary human existence—your qualities, traits, location, culture, etc.—support you in your Soul's Purposes?

From this vantage point, in the company of your MTLOs, take a good look at who you are and consider what could be your next right step in life. Ask for illumination and inspiration to light up the guidance, wisdom, and direction they have for you. Request that your MTLOs shed light on the next best action to close the gap between who you really are and how you are known in the world, based on your awareness that who you are as a human being is optimal for bringing your Soul's Purposes to life!

Ask your MTLOs to facilitate the shift back to the Akasha at large. Retrace your steps. Give yourself a chance to acclimate to your Records. Close your Records by reading the Closing Prayer out loud. Pause to make some notes.

LESSON FIVE

ACTIVATE LOVE & LIGHT

Y ou have been doing a great deal of important work in your Records—transforming your relationship with yourself and others, as well as injuries you have sustained over time. By now, the Light at the core of your being is freer than ever to shine through you, as you, and into your life, which is a blessing for you and us all. Now is a good time to activate love and Light within yourself, to strengthen your awareness of the Truth of your infinite goodness and love of Life. Please join me in the next exercise.

EMPOWERMENT EXERCISE #32
Activating Love & Light Within

Open your Records following the Pathway Prayer protocol. Take a few moments to settle into the Akashic Atmosphere. By now, you are quite familiar with this exceptional spiritual sanctuary, a dimension of Light, Truth, love, and aliveness. As a spiritual realm, it is made of love. That love responds to you and your needs in real time, becoming the precise qualities or expressions of love that support you and make it easier for you to conduct yourself as the loving person you are. Notice the characteristics of this environment. Note the spiritual qualities you find here, such as compassion, kindness, mercy, appreciation, etc.

Open your awareness to the loving presence of your MTLOs. Know that you are the most important focus of their attention. You are their priority—worthy of the guidance and wisdom they have for you. You never see them, but they become more real to you, and with every visit to your Records, you can sense that they are ready to assist you in any way they are able. In your mind's eye, set up a Pillar of Light, approximately an arm's distance in front of you. Do this quickly with the power of your thought. Simply imagine it is there, and it is. Anchor it into the heart of the Earth in any way that makes sense to you. Bring it through the planet and out beyond this dimension, into the cosmos—as far as your awareness allows. Then let it go where it will.

Now, ask your MTLOs to empower you to recognize yourself as they know you. In your imagination, place yourself in the Pillar of Light. Adjust your perception to align with the Soul-level point of view of the Akasha. Perhaps you can get a sense of the love and appreciation they have for you.

Now, expand the Pillar. Bring into your Pillar of Light a handful of your favorite people. This could be your spouse, children, best friends, etc. Make room in the Pillar for all of you to be together in this loving space. Now, be with them in the Light of the Akasha. Open up to the deep and effervescent love shared by this group.

At this time, bring in one person you do not like. Place that individual in the center of those you love. Know that person as they are known in the Light of Truth. Next, bring a group of people you do not like into your Pillar of Light. You may dislike them a little, or you may have strong feelings of contempt for them. This is a group you have a terrible time with. You don't understand them, and they seem to be simply ruining everything. Ask your MTLOs to help you perceive them and know them as they are seen in the Light of Truth. Adjust your awareness to perceive them as Souls—infinite, eternal, immortal beings of love.

Now, let's expand the Pillar and bring in a group of people you have strong, loving feelings for. For some reason, you just love these people. The very thought of them makes you happy. Make room in your Pillar for more love to circulate among those you like and those you do not appreciate.

Finally, expand the Pillar to make room for the entire human family. Perceive them. Know the whole of humanity as they are recognized and known in the Light of Truth. Open your heart to the love emanating from the group and the love activated within you. Notice the urge to love in your own heart and allow yourself to let that love flow. And as you do, there is space within you to receive the love streaming back to you from the entire human family.

Take the Earth and its inhabitants into your loving space with your open heart. Let yourself love planetary life in all its expressions. Hold it close and let yourself be loved in return.

And so, for now, we leave this be. Close your Records, reading the Closing Prayer once out loud. Pause to make notes.

EXPLORE YOUR RELATIONSHIPS

Release Resentments & Embrace
Freedom from Limiting Patterns

This segment of our work is especially meaningful to me, and I hope it will be to you as well. Having examined and addressed your sacred relationship with yourself—resulting in greater inner peace and self-acceptance—now is an ideal time to explore your relationships with others from an Akashic perspective. We will be considering two areas impacting our connection with others: resentment (moving from protection to problem) and freedom from limiting patterns. We know that relations with others are paramount among our time's many significant spiritual challenges. Based on the work we have already done, we know that we are invited to be our true selves in the presence of others, even when they do not understand or appreciate us. At the same time, we strive to allow others to be their authentic selves in our company without our efforts to improve them as we sometimes want to do.

Here on Earth, we have the great privilege of increasing our awareness of the Divine and ourselves through our relationships with other people. Ironically, this dimension is often fraught with conflict and confusion, especially with those we love and cherish. Let's open our minds to the possibility that our difficulties with others may be a path to peace for us. These unhelpful patterns of relating become prominent in what we understand as Karmic Relationships. As discussed previously, Karma is cause and effect. It is a straightforward and natural pattern of life, but often gets stuck or becomes repetitive with negativity. When we have negative opinions or ideas about the pattern or the people involved, that negative pattern persists in our lives. This phenomenon is commonly known as stuck Karma, which can appear between us and another, but in actuality, is always within us.

When we find ourselves in a relationship laden with uncomfortable or destructive behaviors, we should look to ourselves for the solution. It is a supreme spiritual challenge and opportunity to take responsibility for our thoughts, ideas, beliefs about ourselves, others, and particular behaviors, rooting out our critical, harsh interpretations. Making peace with our old, harmful understandings, accepting our choices, and recognizing that we always make selections because they are our best option resolves stuck Karma. We move into acceptance, igniting our release and propelling us into greater personal freedom.

Release Resentments

The journey from resentment to acceptance—from protection to problem—is surprisingly satisfying. Let's examine resentment and find out what it is, the purpose it serves, and how to transform our experience of it. Resentment is a condition of consciousness involving unresolved and festering hurt, anger, or both. It engages our thoughts and feelings. Usually, resentment feels more like hurt than anger. Often we strive to let go of resentment with little success. After understanding the valid reasons for our resentment, our emotions untangle naturally, and we find it possible to release resentment. Initially, we form resentments as protection, but at some point, they become a problem. Many resentments are justified, making them seductive. However, justified resentments are just as damaging as unjustified one.

A most common cause of resentment is having inappropriate expectations of ourselves and others. It's important to expect people to do what they usually do. We may hope and wish they would behave differently, but it is not wise to expect anyone (including ourselves) to act out of character. This only sets us up for disappointment. When we first encounter a shocking loss, betrayal, rejection, or the like, resentment is a wonderful balm enabling us to function despite painful emotions. Our resentment dulls the full impact of an emotional hit, protecting our tender feelings until we gather the strength to face a difficult reality. Over time, however, resentment makes us emotionally and energetically numb, and we lose our sense of aliveness. It fuels our sense of separation and isolation from others and dims our awareness of the Divine. What was once a protective ally becomes a pesky problem.

Having a solid grasp on the Akashic understanding of human motivation and behavior helps us find our way to activate inner peace even when dealing with difficult personalities. Extending the benefit of the doubt is a spiritual practice comparable to the "Of course!" sentiment of unconditional self-love.

It is always easier to examine the Akashic Assumptions before we encounter difficult situations in our relationships. These ideas support extending the benefit of the doubt to others as a way of stimulating our inner peace:

• Everyone is always doing their best to feel better and
  gain experiences of love and inner peace! No one ever
  decides to do less than their best at any given moment,
  but our best is not always that great. The Truth is that our
  motives and actions are always for us, first and foremost;
  this is also true for others. The actions of other people
  are ultimately not against us, even when their actions
  result in hurt and other negative consequences. That said,
  sometimes even our best ideas cause harm to others.

• Do not deny harm or minimize negative behavior. As we
  acknowledge reality—both action and consequences—
  our compassion for our suffering increases, and our
  ability to extend the same to the offending party
  grows. Pretending we are not hurt is ridiculous.

Let's go into our Records and explore this progression. Take this as an opportunity to release resentment and dissolve Karma in a relationship with another.

EMPOWERMENT EXERCISE #33
Releasing Resentments

Open your Records using the Pathway Prayer Process. Now, get comfortable with your MTLOs, your spiritual support team dedicated to your well-being.

In their presence, consider a resentment you have that originated in this lifetime. It may feel reasonable due to injustice. You may have deep, hurt feelings supporting some hostile attitudes toward the offending party. What happened to cause this resentment? Who was involved? What did they do or fail to do? What was your response? How were you affected by the behavior of the other person? Describe what occurred and how you were impacted. Of course you were upset. It is natural to have strong feelings when we are hurt or disappointed. Feeling powerless can unleash deep distress and anger. If you judge yourself for not handling or changing the situation, you may have another layer of resentment toward yourself. It is not surprising that this event caused you so much trouble.

With the guidance of your MTLOs, check to see if you had unrealistic expectations of yourself or another. Were you hoping that they would be different from how they usually are? Did you think you could change them with your love and support? Are you mad at yourself for your inability to stop the transgression? Did you expect yourself to be able to alter the circumstances of the situation?

Ask your MTLOs to help you understand your relationship with this resentment. See how it was so helpful to you in the beginning. Ask to recognize and understand how this resentment protects your feelings and well-being. You would not have grabbed onto this resentment unless it were helping you at the time. So, take a good look to find out how it was beneficial to have this resentment. At some point, there was a shift when this resentment went from being protection to a problem. When did this occur? What was going on? How did you notice this resentment was limiting you in some way? Just observe this. Now, can you acknowledge yourself for having this resentment? It was such a good idea when you first adopted it. Give yourself credit for this powerful method of self-care.

In the compassionate company of your MTLOs, consider that the person who caused you harm was doing their best, trying to grasp an experience of love and peace for themselves. Consider that the harm you suffered was secondary to them. They thought that by hurting you, they would feel better. Does this make sense to you? This entire situation involved people who were valiantly trying to feel better; this includes you. This process may take repeated attempts. No worries—you can always return to this. For now, let this go and turn to other matters.

For this segment, work quickly. Our intention is to awaken to patterns and get a glimpse without getting involved. Do your best; it will be good enough! Bring to mind a time in this lifetime when someone hurt you but did not mean to. It was not intentional, but it caused you pain. Let it go. Let yourself remember a time in this life when you hurt someone else, but you did not mean to. It was not on purpose. You may have felt terrible about it. Let it go. Bring to your awareness a time when another person intentionally hurt you. They meant to hurt you for some reason. Let it go. Let yourself recall a time when you intentionally hurt another person. Maybe you wanted to punish them, or give them a taste of their own medicine, or to teach them a lesson, but it was absolutely on purpose. You may have been very pleased with yourself. Let it go.

Think of a time in this life when you had a very clear idea of what would be good for another person, they followed your advice, and it backfired. Let it go. Remember a time when someone else had a plan for you and your life, and you followed it and were miserable. Let it go. Bring to mind a time in this life when you were certain that you would be happy if you had a particular something (job, person, location, etc.). Then you obtained it and found out it was not what you wanted. Let it go.

Extend mercy and compassion to yourself for all the times you tried to do good for yourself and the people around you, and it did not work out. Extend mercy and compassion to others for all the times they did something hurtful to you in the hope that they would feel better. Consider the possibility that it was their best idea at the time, and they truly believed they would feel better. Let it go.

Close the Records, reading the Closing Prayer once. Pause so you can make some notes.

Practitioner Notes

When working with others as a Practitioner, you are 100 percent responsible for shifting *your* understanding of the situation. Never put any pressure on a client to see or get the Truth. It is your job to recognize deeper Truths and see the essential goodness of your client, no matter what circumstances they find themselves in. As we find clarity, insight, and mercy for our clients and identify the wisdom of choices they made, the shift begins—first within us, then within their Records, and finally within them. Your client may not be able to accept innocence at the level of motive, but as Practitioner, you must. This is the privilege, honor, and responsibility of an Akashic Records reader. Don't be shy—ask for help in the Records when you need it!

Here are some practical suggestions to help you as Practitioner initiate the shift and subsequent transformation:

- Make sure you understand what happened and why your client is upset.

- Accept what has occurred. Accept the response of your client. "Of course!" is the most logical response.

- See the positive value of the resentment. There is always a valid reason for the resentment.

- Strive to understand how the offender was trying to gain an experience of love and peace for themselves. Seek to

understand how the client has been trying to expand
their experience of being loved and safe in the world.

Freedom from Limiting Patterns

Our next area of examination is finding freedom from limiting
patterns. This is important because all humans desire the freedom
to express our innermost Truths and allow Life to unfold. If we
feel thwarted, there must be a good reason for it. Our work is to
discover why we shy away from freedom. With that insight, we
can begin to deliberately move toward what we desire and away
from what we don't want. To move into a greater state of freedom,
we must believe (be convinced by at least 51 percent) that freedom
is good for us. This is because we only and always let ourselves
have what we recognize as beneficial. If for any reason we consider
freedom dangerous or unhealthy, we will make sure not to access
greater freedom because we love ourselves too much to knowingly
harm ourselves.

Freedom requires trust in the moment. If we insist on a specific outcome, then we are not free. If we are afraid and dictate particular
results, we are not free. To be truly free, we must have genuine faith
in the goodness of Life, trusting that whatever unfolds will be beneficial for us in the present. We are required to trust in the goodness of
Life now, not later, or in the future, after we secure a specific outcome.
The good news is that trusting in the moment is quite manageable for
most of us. We can begin experimenting with one sliver of possibility
at a time and let our trust grow.

Most of us are very sophisticated about beliefs. We know that some
are preferred over others. And when asked to identify our beliefs, we
speak the "correct" answers. The problem is that this is not always
what we believe. To uncover our deepest beliefs about freedom, we
need to ask what we know to be true about freedom. It is then that
our true beliefs emerge. Try and let your real beliefs be revealed.

We will do an exercise now to help embrace freedom and activate
greater personal expression without causing trauma.

EMPOWERMENT EXERCISE #34

Embracing Freedom

Open the Records using the Pathway Prayer Process. Consciously connect with your MTLOs in the sacred sanctuary of your Records. Even
though you never see them, you can sense the endless support and
appreciation they have for you. Now, quickly set up your personal
Pillar of Light. Just imagine it is there, a viewing station or screen,
about an arm's distance in front of you. There it is.

Ask to become aware of a lifetime of severe restrictions on your freedom. What kind of freedom was this—Religious? Political? Economic?
It could be any one or combination thereof. Get a sense of who you
were then: your age, gender, family configuration, occupation, interests—approximately when and where and what was going on in your
world, as well as why you were being thwarted. How did you explain
this restriction to yourself as you lived through this life? What did
you think about freedom, and what did you think about yourself?
What decisions did you make about freedom? About yourself? About
the world? Let this go.

Ask to become aware of a lifetime when you restricted the freedom of
others and punished them if they expressed their freedom. What type
of freedom was this—Political? Religious? Economic? Get a sense of
who you were: your age, gender, family configuration, occupation,
interests—approximately when and where and what was going on
in your world, and why you were doing this. We know you would
only restrict others if you believed it was the right thing to do. What
convinced you it was wise to limit the freedom of others? Let it go.

Ask your MTLOs to help you focus on a lifetime when you were
punished for expressing your freedom. Who were you, when, where,
why? What type of freedom? What were the circumstances? What
was the punishment? How did you make sense of this situation? How
did you explain it to yourself? Let it go.

Ask for assistance identifying a lifetime when you had a very positive
experience of expressing freedom. Who were you? When? Where?

What type of freedom? What do you believe made it possible for you to have such freedom? Did the people around you share this freedom? Or were you the only one? What decisions did you make about the value of freedom? What decisions did you make about yourself? Let it go.

See or sense a lifetime when you encouraged others to express themselves fully, to embrace and express freedom. Who were you? When? Where? What freedom did you promote? What made it possible for you to encourage freedom in others? How did things work out for you in that lifetime? How did things work out for the people you encouraged? Let it go.

Ask your MTLOs to help you scan the evolution of your personal growth with regard to freedom throughout your lifetimes. Which ideas are most influential for you in this lifetime? How much freedom are you comfortable with in this life? Let it go. As you take your attention off the Pillar, it naturally dissolves.

Close the Records. Pause so you can make some notes.

And now, my friend, your learning at this Level is complete. And, of course, there is always more to the journey—as we are infinite beings on an eternal quest. But, as humans, it is best to take one step at a time. We have covered a tremendous amount of material. So, give yourself a chance to grow into all that you have been learning, so you become the person you are meant to be. Enjoy who you are and savor the riches of your expanding consciousness. As in previous lifetimes, all you are learning in this life is becoming a part of you. And I know that, at the perfect time, you will blossom, blessing us all.

LEVEL III

MANIFESTING YOUR SOUL'S PURPOSES

A wonderful part of this Akashic Adventure is that it continues! With every stage of my personal journey, I have been led back into this infinite spiritual resource to explore and evolve. When we are in right relationship, there is an ever-expanding quality to the Records.

The purpose of Level III is to empower you to grow in awareness, experience, and expression of your Soul's Purposes so you can identify appropriate ways for manifesting your ideals and your highest potential at this point in this lifetime. By learning to clear obstructions to your Truth, you can find freedom from limiting patterns and discover effective ways to connect your values with the realities of Life. Your dreams and visions of fulfilling possibilities deserve to be brought to life with the support of the insight, guidance, wisdom, and compassion of your Soul as expressed through your Akashic Records.

This Level of the work is based on real-life challenges my students and I have faced in manifesting our Soul's Purposes. As we continue to move through practices in the Records, it is always most helpful to focus on yourself first. You deserve time and attention. Once you absorb and apply these principles and practices, you will become significantly more effective in your work with others. Your diligent efforts will make you a far better Akashic Practitioner and prepare you to work with others in increasingly adept ways. To be recognized as "adept" means you are dedicated, highly skilled, or proficient—considered a professional rather than an amateur. In this case, you are becoming increasingly serious about your relationship with your Soul, as known through the Akashic Records, using the Pathway Prayer Process. You are committed, honorable, and virtuous in your use of the Records for your growth and that of those you serve.

Now is a good time to reflect on your intentions, reconsidering what you hope to gain from participation at each level. Your clarity will help steer you along your path. Your human story is an expression of your Soul's journey. Give yourself a few minutes to center in on your purposes for this segment of the adventure. There is no need to open your Records for this inquiry; just consider this ordinary but important human question and make some notes. What is your intention?

We are all here to increase our conscious awareness of our Soul's Purposes, free ourselves from obstructions and limitations, and discover appropriate and fulfilling ways to express our deepest, most loving inner Truths. As we bring the best of ourselves to life, we expand our capacity to empower others. This lifetime is infused with magnificent Destiny so we can enjoy all the blessings Life has for us! After working through this material, we can all enjoy the process of bringing our Soul's Purposes to life—and be enriched by others doing the same.

Relax and enjoy yourself. Your success is assured. I know you were led to this work by an inner prompting of your Soul precisely because this is *the* lifetime to bring your Soul's Purposes to life! *Now* is your time. Let's begin with a guided meditation for grounding and centering. *You can also access a video of me guiding this meditation here: www .lindahowe.com/Akashic-Meditations.*

AKASHIC LIGHT MEDITATION III

Open your awareness. Bring yourself and all your attention to this place at this time. Set aside thoughts about other things in your life. Concerns about the future can wait. Let yourself be here—in your room, in your seat, here and now—without changing a thing, as this moment is good enough. In this very moment, all of Life exists within and around you. At this time, you are sitting in the fullness of Life *as* the fullness of Life, here in co-creative partnership with the Divine.

Now, direct your attention to the space between the heart of the Earth and your body. Here you find—whether you see or sense—a beam of Light emanating from the core of the planet directly to you, holding you up, supporting you on your journey. Open yourself to allow this ray of Light to shine up into and through you, right up through the center of your being, up into your heart, continuing into your head and out through your crown. As this ray makes its way through you, all the resources the Earth holds for you enter and rise within you. This beam of Light continues on upward all the way upward to the point of Light approximately 18 inches above the crown of your head. You know this place: it is the region where your Soul becomes distinct, individualized as you. It is the realm of the collective, unified Universal Soul, and you are an essential piece of this Soul. It is a paradox and a mystery. You are a part of the whole and, at the same time, complete within yourself.

Here at this level, you will encounter a horizon of Light that is breathtaking in its beauty. As you peer over this horizon, detect visually, audibly, or by sensing that Light is streaming toward you from all directions—in front, behind, on both sides, and above. There is Light moving toward you from places near and familiar, and other places far, foreign, and yet to be discovered. It is the Light of Life, your constant companion. It has been with you since the inception of your Soul, leading, shining the way ahead, traveling alongside you, and even following behind you.

Now, return your attention to the column of Light at the center of your human self. Go back into your body, through your crown, and into the cave of your heart, the intersecting zone of the Light from the Earth and the Light from the heavens. As you move into your heart space, the Light from above follows, streaming into you, flooding your entire being, saturating every molecule, every atom of your being, mixing with the already-present Light energies of the Earth.

Expand your awareness to grasp yourself as the space where Heaven and Earth find harmony, cocreating a dynamic, loving relationship through you, a human being. The finest, highest qualities and characteristics of spiritual Truth are established and expressed through you. You are a focal point of receptivity for Heaven and Earth. You are like a satellite dish, receiving and radiating love to and from everyone you encounter.

Now, expand your sense of yourself from head to toe while staying within your heart space. Allow the infinite, unlimited, eternal, magnificent Light within you to shine out through who you are as a person: in front, behind, and on both sides.

Consider the Light going out in front of you. Watch as it travels out, through, and beyond you into your life, community, and country, following the natural curve of the Earth, shining without effort. And then, from behind, sense the same Light moving through you, your world, your community, and out all over the globe, extending all the way around. The Light shining out through your sides follows the same pattern: through you, into your life, and beyond. And here you sit, the Light pouring through your crown, filling you up, radiating 360 degrees, wrapping itself around the world and all of its inhabitants like a hug.

Once you have embraced the entire planet in Light and love, expand your awareness to another level. Let yourself become aware of the Light of others; let it be supportive and complementary to your own. As your Light extends around the Earth, it meets with others who share a similar consciousness, intention, love, and dedication to the well-being and enhancement of humanity. Connect with other lovers of people, lovers of Life. Make connections with like-minded Souls, some we know, others we will never meet in this lifetime. Our lights combine to form a grid of Light, a weave of layers of Light, penetrating darkness, coldness, and ancient fears—liberating ourselves and others from limiting patterns. No special technique is required. Simply allow the Light to find its way through you; it is infinitely satisfying.

So, here we stand, as points of Light within a greater field of Light awaiting our conscious awareness and contributions. Return your attention to your room, the place you presently occupy on the planet. Open your awareness to yourself as a Pillar of Light within a field of Light. Extend this Light to the walls, front and back, all sides, consciously filling the room with Light perfectly calibrated to who you are and what you need. And together, we reside in an optimal field of Light, supporting and empowering us on this Amazing Akashic Adventure.

And from this place, we begin our work. *And so, we do acknowledge the Forces of Light*. Open your eyes and come into the room. Feel free to light the Akashic Candle as you do this work, reminding you of our hope and desire to be a presence for Light, Truth, and love in the world.

Because this is the advanced course, we are diving in deep spiritual waters! And you are ready. Let's continue on our journey with some powerful exercises.

STRENGTHENING YOUR CONNECTION WITH THE AKASHIC RECORDS

EMPOWERMENT EXERCISE #35
Activating Akashic Awareness

Open your Records using the Pathway Prayer Process. Adjust to being in your Records today, right where you are in this space and time. Here, there is a quality described as the Akashic Atmosphere, governed by the Three Absolutes: *Fear Not, Judge Not,* and *Resist Not.* Note the traits and characteristics of this realm. Commonly recognized loving attributes include peace, safety, compassion, patience, appreciation, and others. How does it feel for you to be here? What emotions of yours are stimulated in this sacred space? Scan yourself and notice if you detect this dimension or energy surrounding you or within you. For some, this is very strong, but for others, it may be much more subtle. Simply observe and note what you find.

Invite the company of your infinitely loving MTLOs. You will not see them now or ever, simply sense their presence. What qualities do you sense when they are around? In their compassionate company, ask your MTLOs for a glimpse of yourself as you are recognized and known from the Light of Truth in your Records. As you observe, notice if you can identify some of the ways in which you experience and express love.

Now, ask for a sense of some possibilities of your Soul's Purposes and your Destiny in this lifetime. Don't worry about the particulars, just a general sense of your purposes. When it comes to bringing your Soul's Purposes to life this time, how does this lifetime fit into the grand scheme of all your lifetimes so far? What is significant for you about manifesting in this life? What are some realistic yet inspiring possibilities for expressing your Soul's Purposes in this life?

Return your attention to your place and close the Records reading the Closing Prayer aloud one time. Pause to make some notes.

With every excursion into your Records, you are no doubt becoming more familiar and comfortable with the Akashic Atmosphere.

EMPOWERMENT EXERCISE #36
Cultivating Spiritual Potential

Open your Records using the Pathway Prayer Process. Take a few moments to center into your Records. Expand your awareness to include the presence of your dedicated MTLOs. You may not see them, but you will sense their presence. In their compassionate company, ask to recognize yourself as seen and known in the Light of Truth or identify yourself as they recognize you. Let's get a general reading on this. You may see images, hear suggestions, or have a felt sense of yourself—all are valid ways to receive guidance within your Records. It may be that you simply sense being in a safe, sacred space, where you are completely accepted as you are, and the core loving goodness inside of you is free to come out into the world.

Now, let's get more specific and look for particular aspects of who you are. As you are held in this Akashic Light, what do you notice as your most vital personal character traits? Get a sense of the strengths and virtues you have cultivated over lifetimes. Focus on the loving traits you have developed over countless centuries.

Direct your attention to how you have learned to listen to yourself, trust your inner wisdom, and express yourself in the world. Notice the treasure trove of wisdom and compassion you hold in your heart/ mind. Here, on this very day, discover all the insights, understanding, and love that you've cultivated for all the ages. All of it is right here within you, now.

Notice the profound commitment your Soul has to you living your magnificence, how your faith and trust in yourself, Life, and the Ultimate Reality have been strengthened in both good and challenging times. Sense your remarkable creativity and the persistent, continuous, deliberate attention the Divine has for you. Open up to this enduring, amazing partnership between your Soul and the Ultimate Reality. Know that there is absolutely nothing you can do to sever this connection. This eternal partnership endures no matter what you do or fail to do, no matter what any other person does or fails to do to you. It is possible to hide from this relationship and minimize or ignore it, but it is an energetic impossibility to disconnect from this sacred bond. Knowing this, take a moment to allow yourself to grasp your unshakeable connection to the infinite, anchored in unconditional love for you now, today, and always.

Close your Records by reading the Closing Prayer out loud. Pause and make notes about your experience.

Strengthening Your Connection to Your Records

The nature of Light is simultaneously radiant and magnetic. As we clear obstructions to our natural radiance, the Light shines through us, as us, out into the world. And simultaneously, by its magnetic property, the Light naturally draws to us that which is ours, whatever we need to bring our Soul's Purposes to life. We do not create, manufacture, or generate Light; Light is already present. The nature of Light is to reach out, beyond, and through all perceived containers and limitations. As we clear away our old limiting ideas, the naturally present Light is free to shine more fully.

Our responsibility is to clear obstructions to the Light, beginning with identifying obstacles and resolving blockages. What are they, and how can they be released? All obstructions and blockages are solidified judgments. Our negative opinions and critical judgments cause stuckness. Acceptance ignites release as a starting point, not as a completion. It may take a bit of time for an obstruction to resolve itself. The process of resolving obstructions and releasing blockage requires:

- Accepting and appreciating our present condition of being stuck;

- Identifying the judgment or condemnation
  we have about a particular issue; and

- Seeing the benefits of the current problem. As we
  appreciate a stubborn pattern for being helpful in some
  way, it will begin to dissolve and ultimately disappear.

Our effectiveness and happiness are greatly enhanced when the link between our inner Light and outer expression is clear. As you recall from the prior levels of learning, five core concepts connect our inner and outer worlds, together forming a Five-Pointed Star of Light. Each of these five concepts has both spiritual and worldly dimensions. As a brief reminder, they are:

- **Incarnation:** To be incarnate is to take human
  form. At this level, we make peace with our human
  self as the optimal agent for our Soul.

- **Authority:** As long as we are here on Earth, there will
  be authority over us. Our challenge is to accept that the
  perfect power of the Divine is transmitted via imperfect
  human beings. Each of us is the author of our own
  universe, but none of us are God of *the* Universe.

- **Discipline:** This is what empowers us to use our gifts wisely.
  It is not punishment! Rather, with discipline, we develop

structures through which energy flows to support our growth and empowerment. As discipline comes from the root word meaning "to listen," a discipline is any activity empowering our ability to hear the voice of Truth within.

- **Responsibility:** Distinguishing true responsibility from false responsibility is one of the most important distinctions we can ever make. True responsibilities to self and others are a crucible for transformation, providing opportunities to let go of limiting patterns and develop inspired approaches and actions for living. False responsibilities are ego- and fear-based; they drain and distract us from our Soul's Purposes. Our true responsibilities are always satisfying, even when difficult.

- **Commitment:** This is the quality of consciousness that empowers us to turbo-charge our path as it unleashes the power embedded in the path, resulting in less obstruction and greater usefulness. As we consciously commit to our path, the path returns to us all the resources of character we need to proceed and fulfill our Destiny.

As we identify and align with the spiritual essence of each core concept, more Light flows. Focusing on these portals to powerful self-expression activates the potentials and promises embedded in our hearts. With this clarity, the Light flows freely into our activities. As a result, we are more fulfilled, and our world is blessed.

Let's do an Empowerment Exercise to upgrade your Five-Pointed Star.

EMPOWERMENT EXERCISE #37
Amplifying Akashic Radiance

Open your Records following the protocol for the Pathway Prayer Process. Settle into the loving, empowering space that is the Akasha. With the guidance of your MTLOs, direct your attention to the Pillar of Light at the center of your being. Start at the root and move up through the trunk of your body and out through the crown of your head. Find a place within the Pillar to center yourself. Sit within the Pillar and look out beyond it, through yourself, out into the world.

Direct your attention and gaze forward. Have your MTLOs guide you to recognize a Pillar of Light directly in front of you and still within your body. This is the Pillar of Incarnation. Take a moment to review your relationship with the particulars of this life. Do you sense any problems within yourself or your family? What if who you are as a person is ideal for demonstrating and expressing your Soul's essence? What if you are your Soul's first and best choice in this lifetime?

Now, move your awareness to the right front of your body, to the Pillar of Authority. Reflect on your general relationship to authority. Do you tend to reject or judge authority? Are you usually fearful of authority? Notice your standard response to authority. Ask yourself whether you are willing to allow imperfect authority figures, such as your parents, to transmit the energy of authority to you. Are you willing to be an imperfect authority to others?

Redirect your awareness to your back body, on the right side, looking out to the Pillar of Discipline. What is your automatic reaction to the idea of discipline? Do you reject it? Do you confuse punishment with discipline? Are you prone to over-disciplining or under-disciplining yourself? Is there a pattern of thought or behavior that would quiet your mind and empower you to hear the inner voice of Truth within?

Next, focus on the left side of your back body, looking out to the Pillar of Responsibility. Note your general response to responsibility. Observe your pattern of true/false responsibilities in this lifetime. True responsibilities transform us into our best selves. False responsibilities deplete us. Notice how you have grown by honoring your true responsibilities.

At this point, let your awareness travel to the left side of your front body, gazing out to the fifth Pillar, Commitment. Notice your "go-to" or default stance. Do you avoid commitment? Or do you become engulfed in it? Ask your MTLOs if there is a commitment you can embrace at this time in your life that will activate the power of your path. Remember, your path can only nurture you once you commit.

Now, bring your awareness back into the central Pillar of Light, the Pillar of Grace. Find a place to rest. Observe the clarity of the pillars; notice how the Infinite Light at the center of your being shines out through you and into the world. No need to send the Light; simply allow it to find its way through and beyond you as it radiates. At the same time, the Light magnetizes what you need to bring your Soul's Purposes to life. Stand as a lighthouse in your world so that you can be easily recognized by everything seeking you.

And so, for now, we let this be. Close the Records by reading the Closing Prayer out loud one time. Pause to make notes.

Spiritual Fitness

One of the most frequent questions I hear from students is, "How can I strengthen my connection with the Records?" Interestingly, being more grounded empowers our ability to accommodate more. Because our human vehicle is a transmitter of Light, we must be reasonably balanced to be effective. We cannot generate or manufacture Light, but we can keep ourselves in a fit spiritual condition. This exercise is designed to empower you to be a more efficient agent for Akashic Light.

EMPOWERMENT EXERCISE #38
Assessing Spiritual Fitness

Open your Records using the Pathway Prayer Process. Begin by taking a few moments to find your center and position yourself in the heart of your Records. As you settle in, open your awareness to the loving presence of your MTLOs. It is amazing that, even though we cannot see them with our inner spiritual vision, we can always detect their presence.

Notice what qualities of love are especially strong today. Safety and security? Or appreciation and enthusiasm? The endless expressions of love come to us in ways that we need on any given day. Pay attention to the combination of qualities expressing love today.

Direct your attention inward, asking, "How am I doing today?" This is a general question, and your response will probably be general as well. You may be "mostly good with a few worries" or have some body aches or pains. It is completely normal to have a combination of conditions occurring simultaneously. Note what they are, being as specific as possible.

Now, focus on your body. How is your body doing today? You may be full of energy or depleted. Maybe you are strong with one particular exception. There are an infinite number of possible responses to this question. Become more aware of the quality of your health. This is a good time to ask your MTLOs for insights into any health concerns you may have. They are always ready to assist with improving our well-being. Remember that they do not directly intervene to change physical conditions but may offer wisdom to us to apply to our well-being.

Next, consider your emotions or feelings. How are you feeling today? Are you happy? Sad? Anxious? Excited? Or some combination of other feelings? Pay attention to the blend of emotions you have today. Maybe you are serene with a bit of worry. Do not try to change what you feel; all feelings are valuable. It is more helpful to identify and name your emotions. Then, ask your MTLOs to help you make peace with all the emotions you have today. They are always waiting for you to ask for their support and give it gladly. And if there is a particular feeling that is very uncomfortable, ask for help resolving that emotion.

At this time, turn your attention to your thoughts. Notice what you are thinking about and the type of thoughts you have. You may be entertaining thoughts of something wonderful, perhaps thinking about someone you love, fostering a happy frame of mind. Or the ideas going through your mind may be negative or angry about something or someone. It is also possible that you are reviewing your fears and making yourself unnecessarily fearful. We always have the power of choice when it comes to our thoughts. We humans have the great privilege of selecting our own thoughts. So, if the ideas in your mind are disturbing to you, stop thinking about them and start thinking about something that makes you happy instead. If you have difficulty changing your thoughts, ask your MTLOs for guidance and support. You are entitled to feel peace and well-being, and you can help yourself by deliberately thinking about pleasing things.

Let's consider the day ahead. The past is over, and the future is not here, so let's think about today. Review your plan for the day, what you expect to experience, things you hope to accomplish, people you want to meet, and any other activities on your calendar. There are likely some things you are looking forward to and others you wish you did not have to do! Ask your MTLOs to empower you to deal with your day—all the activities and people—with love and respect. They are always happy to assist and want to see us succeed.

Finally, ask if your MTLOs have a personal message for you for today, maybe some words or sentiments you can plant in your heart and carry with you as your day unfolds.

And so, for now, we leave this be. Bring your attention back to this day. Close your Records and pause to make notes.

LESSON TWO

THE NATURE OF SOUL, SOUL'S PURPOSES & DESTINY

The Soul is a natural part of who we are, fully aware of our oneness with the Divine. Our inner Divine Spark is a fragment of the Ultimate Reality that contains the wholeness of the Ultimate Reality and reflects Divine Presence through us, as humans, into Life. The Soul is made of love; love is the very substance of the Soul. This is significant as we explore the potential of the Soul and our relationship to it. Because the Soul is made of love, the Soul's Purposes are spiritual, related to the comprehension and expression of spiritual themes, attributes of love. Every Soul's Purpose begins as spiritual; however, because this is a physical plane of existence, a dimension of action and expression, our Soul's Purposes assume physical form.

The individual Soul is a fundamental component of the Universal Soul. While it becomes distinct within each person, it never completely separates from the One Soul—that dimension of consciousness which is fully aware that it is Divine, reflective, and expressive of love, the Ultimate Essence. The Universal Soul's Purpose is unconditional love for self, others, and all of creation; this collective purpose is accomplished one individual at a time. Our primary Soul's Purpose is to consciously learn to effectively experience the unconditional love within, share it with others, and express and enjoy love in our own meaningful way that is unique to us. Every one of us grows into this awareness as our Soul makes its way through human lifetimes. And, as each human can express love, there is a collective ripple of transformation.

Our contribution and participation are essential for fulfilling the Universal Soul's Purpose. Like the moon to the sun, the Soul can be understood in connection with the Ultimate Reality. As the moon is composed of elements capable of reflecting and radiating the light of the sun, the Soul is composed of elements capable of reflecting and radiating the Light of the Divine.

The relationship between Soul and Akashic Records can be confusing at first. Akasha can be understood as the energetic connective tissue linking the Soul to the Source. As such, the Record is related to both Soul and Source, but with its own distinct properties and functions. Although the Akashic Record is the vibrational archive of the Soul, it is not the Soul; it resides at the Soul level of consciousness. Think of it as the invisible correspondent of Soul: the Akashic Record holds the Soul and exists at the level of the Soul. The Soul rests at the floor of the heart center. As the consciousness of the Soul radiates upward in harmony with the Akasha, it connects us to the Source. Another way to think of your Soul is as a photonegative, with impressions made at the inception of your Soul by the Ultimate Reality or Divine Presence. Opening the Records, we shine Akashic Light to reveal the images present and emerging, and stimulate the treasures embedded in the Soul that we have cultivated over our human lifetimes.

Each of us is a co-creative partner with the Ultimate Reality or Divine Presence, with our own opportunities in this role to bring our Soul's Purposes to life here on Earth. Our Soul's Purposes are elements of our Destiny, essential to the permanent component of our Records, which is held in the Akasha and commonly recognized as the "Blueprint of the Soul," even though it is vibrational and invisible. The indelible impression of the Divine Reality in the fabric of the Soul is revealed through our human journey. Understanding this primary principle supports remembering that you are your Soul's first and best choice. All the pieces of the cosmic puzzle are a perfect fit!

As the intersecting zone of Heaven and Earth, the Record is ideal for supporting our efforts to enhance our spiritual awareness here on Earth. This makes it easier to apply spiritual principles to our human living. Since spiritual means loving, we are talking about guidelines empowering us to experience and express love in our lives. We come to each Incarnation with meaningful intentions propelling us to become the most loving human possible. Our intentions are in exquisite harmony with the Universal intention to love ourselves, others, and all creation unconditionally! We manifest these intentions within our regular human selves. Who we are as humans is the ideal convergence between Universal and individual intentions, in precise alignment, for our fulfillment of individual and collective Destiny.

A significant challenge is this: How does our infinite inner being find harmony and fulfillment expressing itself within the restricted circumstances of our human form? As Souls without bodies, we are free and unlimited, infinite. However, as humans, we are finite. This means that every one of us is a living paradox: perfect, infinite, eternal, immortal Souls in imperfect, finite, temporal, mortal human bodies.

Our work is to unleash the infinite love within us for our own benefit and bless everyone we encounter. This spiritual awakening is inspired by our Soul's Purposes, which are to experience, express, and enjoy the infinite love within by discovering the uniquely individual ways we express this love and find meaningful, fulfilling, and valuable avenues for expression of love through service to one another. Spiritual awakening empowers us to be the most loving, generous versions of ourselves.

Now, let's consider how **Destiny** fits into this picture. From the word "destination," meaning a place of arrival, Destiny suggests where we are headed and where we will arrive. Our Destiny is natural to us; it is an inevitable consequence of who we are. The seeds of our Destiny are held within us as our dreams, potential, and possibilities, ultimately connecting us with the world we live in. Destiny happens here in the world but is rarely instantaneous. It occurs through time and within space, actually happening with the raw material of Life.

Made up of converging dimensions, Destiny is composed of our human self, our Soul, and the world in which we reside. Manifesting our Destiny is the inevitable outcome of our Soul being in the world. There is a compelling power natural to our Soul's Purposes—so fierce and inherent in our being that we continue to desire until we begin the process of actualizing these deep inner longings. Even when they do not make good sense, nothing can eliminate our cherished ideals, as they are the Divine seeking expression and fulfillment through us.

Our Soul's Purposes are a natural part of who we are. They are built into our personalities and character, as well as our fondest dreams for ourselves. Yet, many people report that their Soul's Purposes are "no big deal," which is why they do not consider them valuable. Most striking about our Soul's Purposes is that they persist in the face of opposition. We have the talent to realize them, and they self-generate when we move in their direction. The more we grow into them by taking action, the greater our desire and motivation to continue. Born from a place of spiritual purity in our Souls, these Purposes stimulate our experience of being loved, loving, and lovable all at the same time. And the crucible of love births our dreams into reality, giving us the Inspired Manifesting we came to life to experience.

Knowing that our Soul's Purposes are the unique, individual ways we experience and express love, the following clues may help you identify yours.

The Top 10 Clues for Identifying Our Soul's Purposes

1 We want to do what has to be done to realize the goal. Our ordinary desires and interests are very important clues. If we have zero interest in something, it simply is not ours to do. The Universe will not give us a purpose we dread. Our Soul's Purposes are designed to bring us closer to loving, enjoying, and appreciating who we are. They take us into true intimacy with ourselves.

2 We can take the next immediate step, and we have a natural talent
for the goal. Purposes may not be convenient or comfortable, but
we can do what is needed to complete the next step. Ask yourself,
given who I am and what I have today, what can I do? Keep
asking the question, and Life will keep expanding the answer.

3 We enjoy the process even when difficult, demanding, or
inconvenient. There's a myth that our purposes come
easy and require minimal effort. In fact, sometimes
there is bad weather and lots of traffic, and it feels
really hard. Even though our Soul's Purposes require
discipline, responsibility, and commitment, they can
be quite enjoyable and unleash inner happiness.

4 We have enough energy and resources to take the very
next step. We are willing to learn and develop ourselves to
expand our skills to achieve the object of our purpose.

5 We are clear about the experience of our destination
and, at the same time, flexible about how it all comes to
fruition. We understand that Life is our laboratory. We are
fixed about our destination and also flexible about the path
for getting there and open to changes along the way.

6 Perfection is not required. As we pursue our Soul's Purposes,
we encounter obstacles, weaknesses, and imperfections
in our character. Yet, we find ways to relinquish our
shortcomings, overcome limitations, and develop our skills
and talents. The path of purpose refines our character.

7 We stay the course; we cannot quit. Although we may
want to stop, take a break, or put our dreams on pause,
we always return to them. Quitting is not an option.

8 Our purposes have value in and of themselves. We enjoy the
approval of others, but it is not required. Rejections do not stop us.

9 We are willing to begin where we are, act as we are able,
accept assistance as needed, and continue alone if necessary,
with no attachment to time, effort, or resources required.

10 We love ourselves, no matter the outcome. We know that we are an important piece of the connected whole and that, without our contribution, everything will be different. We know that our Soul's Purposes are solely ours to do. The turbo-charged question is some version of this: "Can I love myself... if I succeed? Can I love myself... if I fail? Can I love myself no matter what?"

Let's do an Empowerment Exercise to experience your Soul and discover more about your Soul's Purposes. We will revisit the Zone of Choice, that inner Akashic Realm we visit in between lifetimes to review our progress and make choices about our upcoming Incarnation.

EMPOWERMENT EXERCISE #39
The Zone of Choice

Open your Records following the Pathway Prayer Process. Center into the sacred space of your Records. Open your awareness to the sense of safety, security, reverence, and respect, knowing that the Truth is easier when we feel safe. Ask your MTLOs to assist you in connecting with this infinite, eternal safety. Remember that your MTLOs are totally devoted to you and your spiritual awakening. They welcome your requests for assistance and will never intrude or intervene without an invitation.

Let us begin by exploring your experience of love and your Soul. Invite your MTLOs to direct your awareness to a manageable segment of your Soul so you can examine and get more familiar with it. You may see, sense, feel, or hear something. It may be dim or potent. Just take whatever seems right to you.

Your Soul is spiritual, made of love. What does this feel like to you? Bring in an emotion, which could be inspiring, exciting, peaceful, serene, tranquil, or a combination of various qualities. Then, to the best of your ability, name these qualities and characteristics. What are you finding? And how does this make you feel about yourself? Your life? The big picture?

Now, ask your MTLOs to empower your transition into the Zone of Choice, the realm we visit in between incarnations, where we review our past experiences and make selections for our upcoming Incarnation. Notice the direction of your travel, up or down. Once you arrive, find a place to be, a location to settle in for some examination.

Ask to be reconnected to the time when your Soul, in partnership with the Divine and supported by your MTLOs, selected you as the ideal individual to bring its purposes to life. Why you? What was so compelling, so irresistible about you that your Soul just had to be you at this time? What did you consider to be your most riveting human qualities, your most impressive traits and characteristics?

Given who you are as a person—with all your strengths and weaknesses—what could you possibly be here to achieve, manifest, demonstrate, or realize as the human being that you are? Considering the possibility that you are indeed the ideal candidate for your Soul's Purposes at this time, what might your Soul's Purposes be? (This is a question to ask yourself, not your MTLOs.)

At that time, you had some intentions for yourself in this lifetime. Can you identify any? You also had some expectations. How did you think this life would unfold? What did you expect to occur?

Now, let's focus on your experience of living this life. Consider this lifetime from within your Zone of Choice. Throughout this Incarnation, you have had many moments, episodes, events, and phases when you were flooded with awareness, sensations, emotions, and feelings of love. These moments stimulated or activated the unlimited love within you such that you felt emotional and love poured through you out into your life. Notice what conditions, circumstances, and thoughts ignited these experiences of love awakening within you and moving through you as an expression of Life itself. Ask your MTLOs to help you recognize these powerful times when the love within you just rose up and poured through.

Scan different areas of your life: family of origin, work, creativity, friends, intimate relationships, and health. Observing these, look to see what actions you took activated the flow of love within you.

Now, let's return to the Akasha at large. Retracing your path, you can likely sense the spaciousness of your own Records. Ask your MTLOs to help you identify what activities, people, and places stimulate your awareness of the love inside you. Our Soul's Purposes are designed to bring us closer to loving, enjoying, and appreciating who we are; they take us into greater intimacy with our true selves.

Moving toward manifesting our Soul's Purposes gives us energy and makes us happy. Moving away from manifesting our Soul's Purposes leaves us tired. Pay attention to the simple, ordinary impact of your activities, people, etc., on your level of happiness. Asking yourself some simple questions can help guide this discovery, such as:

- At this time in my life, what gives me energy?

- What makes me want to jump out of bed and live?

- What makes me happy to be myself?

Identifying Soul's Purposes is a process involving thoughts, feelings, and spiritual guidance. Given what you understand at this point, what might be some of your Soul's Purposes in this lifetime?

Make notes with your Records open. When you are finished, close your Records, reading the Closing Prayer out loud one time.

EMPOWERMENT EXERCISE #40
Three-Level Reading for Soul's Purposes

Following the Three-Level protocol we learned in Level II, open your Records using the Pathway Prayer Process. Get settled into your Records in the company of your MTLOs. (For this exercise, write your answers as you go along.)

LEVEL ONE: THE STORY

- How do I understand my Soul's Purposes for this lifetime?

LEVEL TWO: CAUSES AND CONDITIONS

- What factors fuel my quest to know my Purposes and bring them to life?

- What elements of my life experience are encouraging me to manifest?

- Can I understand the relationship between this deep desire and the world in which I live?

- Do my challenges make good sense?

- Do I recognize the positive value of my difficulties?

LEVEL THREE: SOUL-LEVEL TRUTH

- What are the ways that being involved with my Purposes ignites the experience and expression of love in me?

- Do I recognize how pursuing my dreams brings out my very best qualities?

- This inquiry will develop over time. It is perfectly appropriate to repeat this as you grow and change. Your discoveries will continue to deepen and reflect the riches of your consciousness as you travel through your life.

Close your Records by reading the Closing Prayer.

AKASHIC MANIFESTING

To manifest is to make obvious, display, exhibit, or demonstrate. We are always manifesting something; it is our natural relationship with Life. Since we are always involved in bringing something to life, why not deliver what is most satisfying, enriching, meaningful, and fulfilling? Our work here is focused on preferred manifestation.

Manifesting is quite different from magic, which involves using charms, rituals, or spells believed to have supernatural power over natural forces. When we practice magic, we expect an exceptional power seemingly from a supernatural force working outside or beyond natural laws to achieve our desired result.

Akashic Manifesting occurs here on Earth, in real time and space, using earthly materials. This is the only place manifesting can transpire through time as we know it, composed of recognizable materials. Akashic Manifestation means making evident something inspired by Akashic Light and Wisdom through the Akashic Records using the Pathway Prayer Process, which honors natural laws and operates within regular earthly conditions, to make something tangible for the highest good of all.

While it is true that we are ultimately capable of anything and everything, we make selections in the Zone of Choice using specific strengths and weaknesses we have in any given Incarnation. It is simply not true that everything is possible at any moment. While that may be true in other realms, it is false in this world. A more accurate view is to see each lifetime as a sliver of all incarnations in which a well-defined range of gifts, talents, and abilities are available to us.

Our ordinary desires and interests are a very important clue in the process of recognizing our Soul's Purposes. We know something is *not* an option for us in a particular lifetime because we do not want it or have zero interest in it. If we do not want it, it is not ours.

Manifesting happens through us, within the life we live, in the intersecting zone of our hopes, dreams, and wishes as we engage with the world in which we live. In this range, in the crosscurrents of our individual self and the greater world, where our Soul's Purposes take shape.

Requirements for Successful, Preferred Akashic Manifesting

Because the Akasha is the intersecting zone of Heaven and Earth, the Akashic approach to manifesting involves both spiritual and physical aspects. For your manifesting to be fulfilling, it must have elements of both. Your happiness and well-being are required because manifesting moves through you as a human being. Ongoing adjustments accommodate growth. Life is alive. We are alive. Our manifesting is alive. Manifesting is not a one-time event but an ongoing process. We must reevaluate and readjust to stay current in the present and be willing to revise our avenues for expression, so they are appropriate for our life stage.

A simple test can guide us along the path of meaningful, satisfying manifesting. All viable, sustainable manifesting meets the Triangle Test: Heart, Mind, and Will. And so we can bring each item or activity we engage in to our Inner Triangle, asking:

- Does this make me happy? (Heart)

- Does it make good sense to me? (Mind)

- Am I willing to take the actions required
  to bring this to fruition? (Will)

The essential ingredient for fulfillment is love. Our idea or desire must inspire love within us, activate our own experience of love, and encourage us to express love in meaningful and satisfying ways. True spiritual desires inspire us to become the most loving version of ourselves in any given moment. Ultimately, without love, even the best ideas fall flat.

EMPOWERMENT EXERCISE #41
Activating Akashic Manifesting Power

Open your Records using the Pathway Prayer Process. Settle in with your MTLOs, your most trusted advisors. Even though you never see them with your ordinary or spiritual eye, you have developed a precise sensitivity to detect their presence when you engage in your Records. This is a presence you have come to recognize and trust. Relax into this sacred sanctuary of compassion and Truth.

Throughout our work together, you have had some ideas or inclinations about your possible Soul's Purposes. They may not be fully developed, which is fine. We are working with the raw material of new ideas. Note what you think might be some of your Soul's Purposes in this lifetime. You can write down your thoughts or simply make a mental note of them.

This is an important Incarnation for you. It is time for you to achieve remarkable growth and experience Akashic Manifestation. You are here to bring your Soul's Purposes to life and enjoy the process. The number one requirement for igniting your Akashic Manifesting Power is personal happiness. Your happiness and well-being are critical and essential. Do your ideas make you happy? Are they satisfying, fulfilling, inspiring? Does the very thought of any of these possible purposes make you happy?

Does the prospect of moving ahead with any of these ideas make you feel good about yourself? Do they make you feel that you are "good enough" or inadequate? Do these ideas seem a bit impossible for you? Or are they within your reach? Are you inspired by any of these options? Do they cause you to want to learn, examine, explore, and even experiment? Are you willing to take action on any of these even if you are not successful initially? Are you willing to try any of these even if they fail? Can you love yourself no matter what the outcome?

Are you open to adjusting your vision? Are you willing to use your good common sense to modify your purposes?

Some of these questions may trigger a strong surge of insight and information, and even emotion. Others may not resonate at all. Notice which questions are helpful to you now and entertain them. You can always return to this exercise another time to examine other aspects of your dreams.

Now, let's take your favorite possibility to the **Triangle Test**, just one idea at a time:

1 Does this very idea make you happy and feel more loving toward yourself and others?

2 Does it make good sense for you at this time in your life?

3 Are you willing to do the necessary work?

Now, for your manifestation to be powerful, you may have to make some adjustments. This is to be expected. Let yourself adjust your vision of your Soul's Purposes and consider your revised ideal. You can repeat this process as often as necessary. Remember, the top requirement is your personal happiness.

For now, close your Records, reading the Closing Prayer out loud one time. Pause and make some notes. Let yourself absorb your progress and take a rest before we move along to our next segment.

By now, you have a good connection with your Records and are gathering insight about your Soul's Purposes. Please be especially kind to yourself and avoid adding unnecessary pressure. Give yourself a chance to learn. Keep your mind open and your heart soft. Please join me now in an exercise designed to stimulate inner Truths about you and your potential.

Stimulating Inner Truths

Open your Records using the Pathway Prayer. Locate the center region of your Records and get settled. Invite the company of your dedicated team of spiritual advisors, your MTLOs, to be with you. Even though you never see them visually, you have a good sense of them being with you.

In their company, imagine yourself coming into this life as a baby with remarkable potential, full of possibilities for this Incarnation. Ask your MTLOs to shine the Light of the Akasha on you as you enter this lifetime. It may appear to be a spotlight, pure and powerful, with your infant self right in the middle. If you cannot see this image, do not worry. Your imagination is a powerful spiritual tool provided for your support in instances like this. It is perfectly acceptable to imagine this scenario.

Consider your infant self. What do you notice as some obvious possibilities you were carrying in your heart and Soul? These could be anything: a love of music, a talent for building things, a desire to share wonderful meals with people . . . the possibilities are endless. Ask your MTLOs to help you identify some of the dreams, hopes, and wishes you brought into this life. These are some of the particular reasons your Soul, in partnership with the Divine, selected you to make these ideals a reality. Some of your heartfelt desires are on the tip of your tongue; others are buried deep within for safekeeping. Give yourself a chance to consider some of them. Some will be familiar to you; do not expect outright surprises. This is you knowing yourself in the most intimate way.

Now, ask your MTLOs to make it possible for you to get a sense of yourself as a child up until age seven. Again, you might see images or simply feel your child self. Either way is fine. Keeping your child self in the spotlight of pure, powerful Akashic Light, invite your MTLOs to help you glimpse the potential you had as a child. You may be able to observe or get a strong felt sense of your talents, interests, dreams, hopes, and wishes. All of these are important expressions of your Soul's Purposes; none are insignificant! Even when they feel easy and come naturally to you, all purposes have value. Noticing and naming them gives them the respect and honor they are due, and it's a beautiful way to validate yourself.

Continuing through the years, ask your MTLOs to help you recall ideas you have held in your heart for your whole life—things you hope to accomplish, dream about achieving, wish would happen. Some you may have already begun; others are on hold until you are ready.

Continuing through your teenage years into your young adulthood, what did you want to experience in this life? Maybe you took action; maybe you were unable to take action. Either way, those hopes were in your heart. Observe how your relationship with your Soul's Purposes has developed in this lifetime.

Keep the Light shining on yourself and your life up to the present. In the Akashic Atmosphere, where the goodness of everything is understood, let yourself recall those dreams, desires, hopes, and wishes you have been holding. Consider the power of your cherished ideals, particular possibilities that are so precious they have persisted throughout every event of your life. While you have lived a full life with so many experiences, what dreams are still alive within you?

Ask your MTLOs to help you realize how some of your heart's desires have been able to stay alive throughout your life. At times you felt like they were impossible to achieve and tucked them in the far reaches of your mind. At other times, other matters were much more important, and there were even times when you tried to forget them! Notice the persistent quality of a select handful of cherished dreams that have been with you for your entire life.

Yes, it is also true that you have manifested some heartfelt desires. Ask your MTLOs to shine Akashic Light on these. You have brought some of your treasured ideals to life and have been amply blessed by these experiences. Notice how wonderful it is for you when you can manifest some of your most treasured dreams.

At this time, let yourself become aware of the resilient, durable, tenacious nature of your Soul's Purposes. Acknowledge those you have already manifested and those yet to materialize.

And so, for now, we leave this be and close the Records, reading the Closing Prayer out loud one time. Pause to make notes for yourself.

GRIEVANCES & OBSTRUCTIONS TO SOUL'S PURPOSES

am often impressed with the resilient nature of our Soul's Purposes, how they persist in the face of negativity, impossible circumstances, poor health, lousy finances, and so many challenges. Inspired by our beloved, cherished dreams, we endure, no matter what. While it is hard to believe that anything could get in the way of our powerful Soul's Purposes, it happens. Let's see what we can discover about the value of obstructions—and how to grow beyond them.

Recall that permanent, sustainable transformation, or healing, requires us to address both inner and outer aspects. In this area, we recognize obstacles or obstructions as outer aspects, and grievances or complaints against the self as inner aspects. For complete freedom, we need to address and resolve both grievances and obstructions. Once we can dive into our deep inner reservoirs and release stuck traumas from other lifetimes, we can launch our understanding of and relationship to manifesting. This inner work will make our external actions significantly easier, which we all deserve.

Let's begin with the inner aspect, grievances. Complaints against ourselves can hold us back from realizing our dreams. A grievance is a cause for distress providing a valid reason for complaint (an expression of grief, pain, or dissatisfaction). Self-condemnation, or rejection in any form, will always prevent us from experiencing our potential. Negative judgments keep us attached to the object of our disdain. For example, if we think we are stupid, we are stuck with being stupid, even if it is not true. While we may have valid reasons for our angst, it is never helpful to hold grudges against ourselves. Better to acknowledge our failings, apologize if appropriate, and move on. Sometimes we are here to learn to love ourselves in the experience of failure and disappointment.

Acceptance (not to be confused with approval) facilitates release, freeing us to move along our life path. As we accept and allow ourselves to be who we are, precisely the way we are, we initiate freedom from old restrictions and move toward manifesting our dreams. The opportunity here is to get on your own side, no matter what you have done or failed to do. Find a way to align with yourself, even if you are not especially pleased with your behavior or predicament. Stretch to understand your reasoning. Remember that we always make choices that we believe will activate an increased experience of love—no exceptions.

Obstructions (blocks or obstacles) are slightly different from grievances as they present "outside" of us. They impede, hinder, thwart, or interfere with our intended actions. With this inspiring, lifelong dream within our Soul, what could possibly be in our way and why? There must be positive, valid reasons obstructing us from proceeding with our desires. When facing obstacles, it is worth considering whether I am being honest with myself. Is this my dream, or does it belong to m,y parents or spouse? It is helpful to remember that harsh judgment always stops us. Whether focusing on ourselves or the obstacle, condemning something or someone will always bring us to a stop.

Maybe we believe it is more spiritual to be deprived or that it is better to be happy even though we are miserable and sad. No outside force wants to deprive or punish us for appreciating our own good. Likely, we do not have what we want because we are afraid to have it. We only allow ourselves to have what we want when we are convinced that it is in our best interest. What's more, is it possible that our obstructions are somehow helpful? What happens if we reconsider our obstructions and look for all the good reasons they exist? Is there some good reason why we do not yet have the objects of our desires?

Thinking about your most treasured dream for yourself, the obstacles you have encountered, and grievances you have against yourself concerning this dream, let's do an exercise in your Records to shift your relationship with these obstructions.

EMPOWERMENT EXERCISE #43
Shifting Your Relationship to Obstructions

Open your Records using the Pathway Prayer Process. Relax into the sanctuary of infinite kindness, respect, and understanding that is your own Akashic Records. Open up to the presence of your protective, generous, committed MTLOs, who are always ready to support you in practical, spiritual ways.

In their company, describe your favorite, most cherished dream for yourself in this lifetime. It is best to contemplate something very meaningful to you, something you have wanted for your whole life. Please keep your focus on this lifetime. When did you become aware of this possibility? What is it? Describe what you want in conversation with a trusted friend, telling them what you hope to experience in this life. Continue to share with your MTLOs the plans you have made so this dream happens, describing the actions you have taken, including the failures you have had, as well as your successes.

Survey your journey with this distinct possibility—this Purpose of your Soul. What do you recognize as obstructions to success? What interferes or prevents your fulfillment of this desire? Perhaps you are lacking some skills or education that would be helpful. What are you afraid of? What traits, characteristics, qualities, or conditions within you are thwarting your dreams? What complaints do you have about yourself? Are you holding some grudges against yourself? Is it possible that you could achieve your dream even with this imperfection? What if you have this flaw for the rest of your life? Is it conceivable that you could realize your dream even though you are not perfect? Are there people, places, or circumstances outside of you that are hindering you? Identify any possible perceived, external obstacles to manifesting your dream.

Now, let's imagine that these obstructions are helpful, guiding or directing your quest. Consider that you arranged for these hurdles for some very good reason. You love yourself and are constantly striving to provide more love for yourself. How is it possible that these obstructions somehow assist you on this journey? Ask your MTLOs to empower your perception so you can sense a way in which these obstructions have been your trusted allies, helping you become more loving in this life.

We are going to shift gears just a little bit. Throughout your life, you have made some decisions that have not brought about your desired results, perhaps causing you to be upset with yourself. With regard to this particular heartfelt dream, bring to mind some choices you made that led you away from your desire rather than toward it. You may have done something you are unhappy about or avoided taking action when it would have brought your preferred intention to fruition much sooner.

With the assistance of your MTLOs, notice if you had any other viable options at the time. Can you sense that your selection was the best idea you had at the time? Something about it was compelling. What drew you to make this choice? Consider how your response was helpful at the time. Do your best to be compassionate and understanding with yourself. If you have difficulty being sincerely kind and respectful of yourself, ask your MTLOs for help.

Are you willing to treat yourself with respect and dignity even though you are not perfect? Are you open to manifesting your dreams even though you are imperfect and sometimes make mistakes? Are you willing to love yourself and others and participate fully in life, even though you have not yet manifested your treasured Soul's Purposes?

And so, for now, we leave this be and close the Records. Pause to make notes.

Releasing Stuck Traumas

You may be curious why we do not "do" anything with what we discover in these Empowerment Exercises. In this work, we allow the Akashic Light to initiate changes; our relationship to everything transforms with shifts in awareness. As we recognize core Truths holding our patterns in place, those that no longer support us begin to dissolve, opening the way to new possibilities. The work we do is in the realm of awareness, and it is deceptively simple and radically powerful!

Underneath all of our conscious activity with regard to manifesting is a wealth of universal concerns we have adopted through the course of our many lives. In this segment, we steer our attention to releasing stuck traumas we've experienced in other times and places and confront universal fears about living and dying that are affecting us at this time. Sometimes these collective concerns affect us knowingly, other times without our consent. For example, fears about living can result in difficulty starting things, especially those that are important. In fact, fears about death can bring about resistance to moving along or completing projects. In this next exercise, we will examine the full range of possibilities so you become aware of your stumbling blocks and recognize ways to move beyond them.

In this next Empowerment Exercise, we will use the chakra system as portals of consciousness. This is not an entire course in the chakras. You are not expected to know anything about them for this to be effective. Just follow along to the best of your ability. You have all you need to proceed.

EMPOWERMENT EXERCISE #44
Moving Beyond Ancient Fears

Open your Records using the Pathway Prayer Process. Settle into your Records in the loving company of your MTLOs. Ask them to help you sense the sphere of Light surrounding you and the Pillar of Light within you, which is anchored at your root and extends out through the crown of your head. This inner Pillar holds the major energy centers within you, your chakras, in place. Although you may never see them, they are constantly working to maintain the flow of the Life force through you.

Now, invite your MTLOs to assist you in recognizing how you carry ancient, universal fears of living and dying. Perhaps you are anxious about starting new projects, preferring instead to continue with familiar activities even when they are no longer satisfying. You may do this with your work or even in relationships. Maybe you are comfortable starting things, but you stop and move on to something else when they become difficult. Or perhaps you are afraid that your ideas will be harmful to yourself or others and find it easier to pretend you do not want to move forward because you do not want to inconvenience anyone. Just get a sense of your general pattern with regard to initiating new projects or pursuing your dreams in this lifetime.

Ask your MTLOs to assist you in recognizing your customary behavior about completing projects. For example, you may dread finishing and do all kinds of things to prolong a project or keep a relationship going, even though no one is happy. Or you may find yourself rushing to finish and becoming sloppy with the details. Some of us avoid completing or fulfilling our dreams; others simply hurry to finish up whether our project is ready or not. Again, we want to get a general sense of your standard pattern around completing projects or fulfilling your dreams.

Now, ask your MTLOs to empower you to enter into the inner Pillar of Light at the core of your being. Direct your attention to its entry point at the base of your physical body. Here, ask your MTLOs to open up the root chakra so you can explore the birth experiences that had the most impact on you in this life. Here you will find that you have had a great variety of experiences being born—some were easy, elegant, and graceful. You had lifetimes of excitement about being born and others full of dread. You had lifetimes knowing you were coming into loving, healthy experiences and others that were troublesome and even difficult. Sometimes, your mother was young, healthy, and strong, and she had an easy birth. And, other times, your mother was sick or frail; she did not survive the delivery. We all have a full spectrum of birth experiences.

Ask your MTLOs to help you identify a birth experience that negatively influences you in this life. Note the circumstances. What happened? How did you respond? What decisions did you make about yourself? About Life? Maybe your mother died, and you felt so terrible that you decided you would never do anything to upset anyone—and so you have been unable to manifest your dreams. Whatever occurred, can you extend love and compassion to yourself?

Now, let that experience go. Look for a positive birth experience—one in which you were delighted, as were your parents. You felt you were bringing love and coming home to a completely loving environment. It was wonderful. Take a moment to allow yourself to feel how magnificent it was to be so conscious of the infinite love within and around you. At this time, let this infusion of love permeate every cell of your being.

Let the experience go, but let the love remain. Take a deep breath. Ask the MTLOs for assistance as you allow your awareness to travel to the crown chakra, the top of your head. This is the point of departure or death. Ask your MTLOs to stimulate this energy center—the one holding the memories of all the deaths you have ever had—so you can find which ones are most influential in this Incarnation.

As with your birth experiences, you have had every type of death imaginable. In some, you were surrounded by peace and love; your passing was painless and graceful. At other times, you died suddenly, maybe as a youth or even as a middle-aged person. In some lifetimes, you were elderly, quite sick, and all alone when you passed. There were lifetimes when you were tired and grateful to be moving along to your next experience. And, of course, in some lifetimes, you were heartbroken when you had to leave.

Ask your MTLOs to help you recognize a death experience that has a negative, limiting impact on you in this lifetime. Notice the circumstances. What happened? How did you respond? What decisions did you make about yourself and Life? Maybe you determined that Life was not fair, and it was better for you not even to bother participating. Or, you felt that it was too hard, too painful, and so you would rather not take any chances. You may have died in war with overwhelming feelings of hopelessness. There are so many possibilities. The critical question is: Can you love yourself even though you were in a terrible situation? Can you love yourself even though you died in such a tragic way?

Now, let that go. Turn your attention toward another death experience, a positive one. Ask your MTLOs to help you identify a positive death, one in which you were at peace, unafraid, and willing to go to your next Incarnation. You may have been alone or with loved ones, but you were totally clear about the love in your own heart and the love circulating throughout every life circumstance. You were confident in the reality of love. Take a moment to allow yourself to relish this experience. Knowing that love would never die, you felt you were a being of love in a sea of love. It was marvelous. Let your understanding of the situation fall away, but allow the love to remain.

Move now into the cave of your heart. Let your awareness of the inner Pillar fade away, your recollection of difficult passages at birth and death dissolve, so that all that remains is love: you, a being of love, in a universe of love, unconditionally loving yourself through hardships and joys. In so doing, let the limitations of ancient difficulties dissolve—and you, my friend, are free.

And so, for now, we leave this be and close the Records, reading the Closing Prayer out loud one time. Pause to make some notes.

MANIFESTING YOUR SOUL'S PURPOSES

Many people are hyper-focused on manifesting these days. Even if you are basically content, folks around you are clamoring for authentic, fulfilling manifestation. It is the nature of Life to constantly expand, so it makes good sense that, once we achieve a goal, another one comes to our attention. This is not an indication of a problem, but rather evidence that we are alive, growing, and in harmony with the nature of Life.

For those dedicated to awakening spiritual awareness, we came to the planet at this time precisely to actively participate in an epic collective leap of consciousness by contributing our manifestation of Soul's Purposes to the collective wave of change. Each of us has a significant relationship with manifesting our Soul's Purposes. Our clearing work enhances this intimate experience and expression. Clearing in the Records involves recognizing truth, accepting and allowing ourselves to exist, and making peace with imperfection. As we take these steps, our deepest desires come into focus, making our connection with the world in which we live much more harmonious. It gets easier to live out our dreams! All the goodness of Life is within you, including your dreams, which means you are the optimal person to manifest your dreams. Yes, you are the ideal individual to experience, express, and enjoy your dreams. It is a universal law that the desires of our hearts are given to us because we are the ones who can bring them to life! Once we make peace with who we are—including our experiences, blockages, and perceived imperfections—our deepest Destiny emerges. And when our conscious understanding catches up to our ideals, then our dreams begin to come true.

To manifest, we must believe that manifestation is in our best interest; at least 51 percent of the self must be convinced that our desires are beneficial for us. We only allow ourselves to be, do, and have those things we deem good. While we may think manifesting sounds like a great idea, we still may have some old ideas lurking around, preventing our ability to bring about change. In our next exercise, we'll explore this topic.

EMPOWERMENT EXERCISE #45
Recognizing Personal Patterns & Beliefs

Open your Records using the Pathway Prayer Process. Consciously connect with your MTLOs. Set up your personal Pillar of Light. Simply think it is there, and it is there, about an arm's distance in front of you.

Ask your MTLOs to become aware of a lifetime when you had strong desires to manifest your Soul's Purposes but were severely restricted or totally stopped from doing so. Get a sense of who you were, what was going on, and why you were thwarted. How did you explain this conflict to yourself as you lived through this lifetime? How did you live with this limitation? What were your thoughts about manifesting your Soul's Purposes by the end of this life?

Ask to become aware of another Incarnation, one where you were active and successful in squashing the manifestation of others. Get a sense of who you were, approximately when, where, and what was going on. For example, we know you would only restrict others if you believed it was the right thing to do. So, what convinced you that it was the best thing for you and everyone else to prevent people from manifesting their desires?

Now, ask your MTLOs to help you identify a lifetime when you successfully demonstrated your Soul's Purposes and were somehow punished. Let's get a sense of who you were, when and where, what you were manifesting, and how you were punished. How did you explain this situation to yourself?

At this time, ask for assistance recognizing another lifetime where you had a particularly positive experience of manifesting. Who, when, where, and what was the nature of your manifestation? What happened that made this so positive for you? Were you the only one, or did others have a similar experience? How did you explain this occurrence to yourself? What did you believe made it possible for you to enjoy such a positive experience? Based on this favorable experience, what decisions did you make about the value of manifesting your Soul's Purposes? What decisions did you make about yourself?

How about a lifetime when you actively encouraged others to seek and initiate the process of bringing their Soul's Purposes to life? Who were you? When? Where? Why? What did you know or believe to be true—whether about people or manifestation? What convictions did you have that made it natural for you to empower manifestation in others? How did that lifetime turn out for you?

Ask your MTLOs to help you scan the evolution of your relationship and your understanding of manifestation throughout your Soul's journey. Which ideas are most influential in this lifetime? How many manifestations are you comfortable with at this point in this life?

Let this all go and collapse your Pillar of Light. And so, for now, leave this be and close the Records. Read the Closing Prayer out loud one time. Pause to make some notes. This has been a very productive session. Please make sure you get some fresh air, take a walk, and then let yourself rest. You are a courageous Soul in the midst of a powerful growth process.

As a result of our work so far, you are well prepared to address issues of cocreation, fertile conditions for manifesting and making conscious choices—all supporting your relationship with money. The purpose of this exercise is to activate your co-creative partnership with your Records.

EMPOWERMENT EXERCISE #46
Activating Your Co-Creative Partnership

Open your Records using the Pathway Prayer Process. Return to your comfortable, familiar place within your own Records. Settle into that sacred space where it is easier for you to become aware of the deep spiritual Truths about yourself. Of course, your MTLOs are present even though you cannot see them; you can feel that they are right there with you, ready to support you in any way they can.

In their company, bring to mind some of your thoughts about your Soul's Purposes in this life. Note the most captivating possibilities. Notice which one is most inspiring to you at this time in your life. Describe this idea to your MTLOs. Share the idea itself: what it is and how you think you can accomplish it. Observe your emotions as you are in conversation with them. Does describing this Purpose bring you happiness? Excitement? Deep inner peace? Which emotions are stimulated in you as you consider this particular Purpose of your Soul?

The MTLOs are your most trusted spiritual advisors, so if you are struggling with the idea, ask for their help. Perhaps your original idea needs to be modified. When we are engaged with our MTLOs, inner peace is always available. When we are disturbed, it is an indication that our ideas need to be revised a bit. If adjustments are necessary, what modifications will make this a fulfilling experience for you? Go ahead and alter your idea until it feels like a perfect fit for you!

Now, as you ask your MTLOs for insight and guidance about this Purpose, they may have questions for you. They want to empower you to manifest your Purposes. What suggestions do they have for

you? Do they have any recommendations about how to best proceed? This discussion is designed to help you explore a specific
Soul's Purpose. Let them help you understand the Purpose and how
to make it real.

At this point, ask them to help clarify the particular ways in which
they will help you as you go forward in bringing your Soul's Purposes
to life. Since they will not do it for you, nor will they give you supernatural powers or change your essential human makeup, what can
they do to help manifest your Soul's intentions? Usually, they relish the opportunity to encourage us. They are totally dedicated to us
becoming the most loving, fulfilled versions of ourselves. And they
honor who we are as human beings. So they never make inappropriate suggestions; whatever they recommend is always within our
capabilities. If it seems like your MTLOs are encouraging you to do
things that are impossible (such as spending money you do not have),
then say, "No," and ask again. Remember, you are an equal partner
with your MTLOs. If, for some reason, you find yourself shy about
speaking up in this relationship, then ask for support. If you do not
feel you are an equal or valued partner, then bring this to their attention and ask for guidance in this matter. They are counting on you
to be your best self in this relationship and are happy to support
you with insight, guidance, and wisdom.

Now, let's find out what they expect you to do to fulfill your Soul's
mission. They may want you to learn something new, take a specific
action, or perform any number of activities. Since the MTLOs do not
have bodies, they need us to make spiritual reality tangible here on
Earth. What are they counting on you to do?

By now, you have a better sense of your co-creative connection with
your MTLOs. There are things they cannot do and other things you
need help with. Together, the rich, spiritual wisdom and compassion
living in you can be delivered to the world in ways that are meaningful and satisfying to you and everyone you encounter. You are
naturally better together. And so, for now, we leave this be. Close the
Records, reading the Closing Prayer. Pause to make your notes.

Robust Manifesting

We all want our manifesting to be powerful, intentional, and enthusiastic—robust. Considering this matter from within the Akashic Realm, we gain a perspective fueling the quality of the manifesting for what we deeply desire. From the Akashic point of view, we observe the profoundly obvious: that manifesting occurs here on Earth, through us precisely as we are in the present, in time and place as they are understood on this planet. If our manifesting happens outside of ordinary time and place, then it does not matter to us, and it is not real or tangible. We are moving away from ancient superstitions and beliefs into fashioning our spiritual values into recognizable physical forms. Some environments encourage this kind of manifestation and others make it very difficult. Let's consider what fertile conditions might be when it comes to worldly success and manifesting our Soul's Purposes.

One feature of fertile conditions is supporting our accelerating vibrations while we stay grounded. Maintaining our grounding amid a quickening makes our work more effective and lasting, which is ideal for most of us. It is also important to recognize that we shift from habitual, unconscious manifesting into preferred, intentional, desirable manifesting. And there is a world of difference between them! Our habitual manifesting is also our default setting. We all have a natural bottom line that we never drop below. Even on the worst days of our life, we can be reasonably certain that there are some conditions we will meet. This habitual manifestation is fine, but we are interested in preferred manifestation, which requires greater conscious awareness and action.

Humility, Patience, and Peace are all ingredients that contribute to fertile manifesting conditions. Humility comes from the Latin word *humilitas*, referring to the Earth, being from or of the Earth, being grounded. We are "of the Earth." Water makes up 70 percent of Earth's surface and 70 percent of the human body. 99 percent of the human body is comprised of just six elements found in the Earth: oxygen, carbon, hydrogen, nitrogen, calcium, and phosphorus. The fact that humans share these essential, common elements speaks volumes about our naturally harmonious relationship with our planetary home.

Although we play different roles in the cosmic drama, we are part of the same universal production.

Humility and humiliation are easily confused and decidedly different in origin and expression. Humiliation is rooted in shame and worthlessness—diminishing our ability to harness and share our inner gifts. On the other hand, humility is anchored in love and acceptance, accurate self-assessment, and appropriate appreciation. With genuine humility, we are propelled to share our gifts with the world in the best way possible, even while knowing we are not perfect. Our human frailties do not hold us back; we are not ashamed of them.

The next critical distinction is between special and unique. Special is rooted in humiliation, demanding undue praise to soothe a damaged ego. It separates us from each other, manufacturing a false hierarchy of self-importance. Uniqueness assumes we are all of equal value with varying gifts, talents, and abilities. Based on true humility, everyone comes to the game of Life aware of their strengths and weaknesses, and choosing to participate for the good of the whole. Participation and contribution are based on giving. In the case of humiliation, participation is rooted in getting validation, recognition, or other human acknowledgment. The stronger we are rooted in humility, the easier it is to stay grounded, remaining aware of our humanity while the Light within accelerates our frequency. Faster vibrations cause rapid transformation with far less effort. This is most helpful once we've established our intentions, so we do not bring about more of what we do not want! So, take a few minutes now to make sure you are clear in your heart and mind about what you want before we proceed any further.

Let's get a sense of the role patience plays in manifesting. Patience is the ability to exhibit self-control and maturity: to remain calm, constant, and steadfast as change happens. Timing is very important in manifesting. Patience bears discomfort without complaint. If we act before we are ready, then we will fail. If we wait too long, we miss opportunities. When we patiently allow our dreams to fully develop for us personally and for the world, we are well received. There is a precise alignment between our Soul's Purposes and the rest of the world. What you want to bring is what Life needs, all at the correct time! Therefore, we manifest our Soul's Purposes now, in earthly time.

Peace promotes Akashic Manifesting by nurturing the development and growth required. Peace is an accepting quality of consciousness characterized by safety, calm, and serenity; it is the absence of judgment, tension, and strife. Energetically, peace is neutral; there is no push/pull in the presence of peace. There is simply an allowing. (In contrast, the energy of fear is pulling, and the energy of anger is pushing.)

Let's do some work in your Records to raise your vibration so you can more easily receive your dreams.

EMPOWERMENT EXERCISE #47

Raising Your Vibration

Open your Records following the protocol for the Pathway Prayer Process. Take a moment to consciously reconnect with your MTLOs. Invite them to join you in this exercise, where our goals are cultivating conditions for accelerating your vibration, strengthening your core strengths, and preparing you to receive your dreams.

Let yourself sink into the Earth, imagining that you are decomposing so that the molecules of your body find their counterparts in the Earth, and feel your innate connection with the same elements that make up this planet. Give yourself a moment to rest and rejuvenate, and then draw energy up from the Earth when you're renewed and invigorated. Feel yourself standing on the face of the Earth, rising up, very much a part of it all, and yet also a unique, individual expression of Life. Feel yourself at peace, with a true sense of humility.

Now, ask your MTLOs to make it possible for you to identify your relationship with time in this life. Gather some understanding of your general patterns concerning time. Is time too fast for you? Too slow? Or just right and in sync? Does your sense of time change in different circumstances? Are you normally patient? Or impatient? In which situations do you tend to have more patience? In which situations do you have less patience?

With regard to manifesting your Soul's Purposes, do you trust the natural growth process of your projects? Do you have any trouble believing that you are an essential slice of Life within the whole Universe? Does it make sense that your Soul's Purposes are important to the Universe?

It is entirely possible that manifesting your dreams will take a long time. Is that okay with you? On the other hand, it is also entirely possible that manifesting your dreams will happen very quickly. Is that okay with you? Ask your MTLOs to empower you to appreciate the ideal timing Life has for you and your purposes.

And now, in the richness of true humility, with respect for the reality of earthly time, open your awareness to the presence of peace—both a fundamental quality of the Akashic Atmosphere and an essential element of you! You are the only human being residing in the heart of your Akashic Records; like the yolk rests in the field of the egg white, you rest in the Akashic Atmosphere. In your mind's eye, dissolve the boundary between yourself and the Record. Let your inner peace flow into the Akashic Field, and let the peace of Life as it exists in the Akashic Realm flow into you. Feel nurtured and unified with the power of peace both within and beyond you. It is your well-earned gift.

Any one of us can indeed be very gifted or have an inspired idea to bring to the world, but harnessing our talents is extremely difficult in times of turmoil. The greatest creative achievements in the arts manifest during times of peace. Similarly, your personal peace powerfully prepares you to receive your heartfelt dreams. Ask your MTLOs to help you recognize one way you can enrich your experience of inner peace and trust to prepare the way for your magnificent manifestation. And so, for now, we leave this be and close the Records. Pause and make some notes.

Worldly Success & Spirituality

To begin this section, let's clarify some basic terms:

- **Money** is a medium of exchange.

- **Abundance** means having more than enough; amply
  sufficient, copious, plentiful, ample, bountiful, and rich.

- **Prosperity** is the condition of thriving.

- **Prosperous** means success, especially economic well-being;
  financially abundant circumstances; flourishing; favorable;
  auspicious; comfortable; well-fixed and well-to-do.

Let's start with money; money represents an energy exchange. In most
of the world, we trade our energy, in the form of our gifts, talents,
and abilities, for money. The circulation of money is a manifestation
of our interdependent relationships with others around the globe, a
reminder that we are part of the whole of humanity. Since none of us
can do or provide everything we need—nor should we—we are here
to discover ways to interact and engage, to give and receive, to find
our true place in the Circle of Life.

Money is a means of exchange, supporting us in manifesting our
Soul's Purposes. Think of money as a tool that helps express our Soul's
intentions. There does seem to be some confusion about money as
an indicator of Divine favor—some people believe that wealth is evidence of God's love. Others believe that poverty is inherently spiritual.
Neither belief is true; our financial condition is not a moral issue.
Wealth and poverty are simply conditions of life inviting us to relinquish our judgments, love each other unconditionally, and participate
and contribute to the best of our ability.

Perfection is not the goal. The purpose of increasing spiritual
awareness is to manifest a life of enriching usefulness, to accelerate unconditional love for the self, others, and all of creation. The
Universe is seriously invested in each of us awakening to our lovabil-
ity and value. It will always provide the resources we need to bring
forth the very best of who we are, so we can effectively participate in

life and deliver the contribution we carry in our hearts, for our happiness and that of others.

We are always satisfied by what is ours to do and never fulfilled by what is not. There is just never enough of what we do not genuinely want and always more than enough of what we truly desire. The Akashic Record is an ideal realm, emotionally safe and loving, for us to explore, examine, and experiment with our values and Truths. Self-honesty is paramount.

Here's a very relevant exercise, designed to interrogate your relationship with money.

EMPOWERMENT EXERCISE #48
Shining Akashic Light on Your Relationship with Money

Open your Records using the Pathway Prayer Process. Establish your personal Pillar of Light about an arm's distance in front of you. Simply think it is there, and there it is! Consciously reconnect with your MTLOs.

Begin this time by taking a quick glimpse at your infant self when you first arrived on this planet in this lifetime. It is perfectly acceptable to imagine this. How much cash did you have when you arrived? Include any investment, property, inheritance. Now, ask your MTLOs to make it possible to see how much money you will take with you into the next life.

Let this go and redirect your attention to your personal Pillar. We will be working rapidly in this exercise; just stay with it to the best of your ability. Ask your MTLOs to give you a sense of a lifetime when you had tremendous wealth bestowed on you by virtue of your royal birth, and you totally enjoyed it! Let that go. Now, see a lifetime when you had great wealth by virtue of your royal birth, but it was a terrible burden to you. Let it go.

Ask your MTLOs to help you recognize a lifetime when you were born into dire poverty—perhaps into slavery or a caste system—but it did not bother you. Let it go. And now, a lifetime of being born into hopeless poverty—serfdom or slavery—where you suffered terrible self-loathing or deep resentment for wealthy people. Let it go.

Ask now to recall a lifetime of working hard to attain wealth when you were very pleased. And another lifetime of tireless effort to attain wealth but in which you were very unhappy. Ask your MTLOs to help you identify a lifetime of dramatic swings in fortune. Perhaps you were a farmer who had to deal with unexpected weather or a shipping magnate who faced storms. Either way, you were not bothered. Now ask your MTLOs to help you identify another life of extreme swings in fortune that caused you profound emotional distress.

See a lifetime of resenting people with money and glorifying poverty. And a lifetime of glamorizing people with money and holding contempt for those in poverty. Your MTLOs can assist you in recognizing a life of religious justification for wealth. And another lifetime when you experienced a religious justification for poverty.

How about a lifetime of stubborn unwillingness to use money to bring your Soul's Purposes to life? And a lifetime of appropriate distribution of funds to ensure that your Soul's Purposes were brought to fruition. Now, let this all go.

Turning to this lifetime, ask your MTLOs to help you identify your dominant pattern around money. Most of us have a combination of restriction and freedom, a sense of "enough" and "not enough." Ask to get a sense of what it would be like for you to have unlimited funds. What do you like about this? What do you dislike? Now, what would it be like if you had zero funds? What do you like about this? What do you dislike? Can you love and enjoy yourself and others if you do not achieve great wealth in this life? Can you love and enjoy yourself and others if you do achieve great wealth in this life?

Looking over your life, can you see any connection between your Soul's Purposes and your cash flow? How much money do you need at this time to take the very next step in bringing your Soul's Purposes to life? What do you have to offer that makes you so happy that the Universe actually pays you?

Allow your personal Pillar of Light to collapse. And for now, we leave this be and close the Records. Pause and make some notes.

SPIRITUAL SUCCESS

S uccess, as used here, means a favorable or desired outcome: gaining wealth of every variety or a recognition of valuable contribution. Spiritual success involves love: recognizing, experiencing, expressing, and enjoying the infinite love within us in ways that are meaningful and fulfilling. The giver is nurtured by a love of giving. This kind of spiritual giving is not to be confused with old ideas of sacrifice. Sacrifice is letting go of something precious in exchange for a better, more satisfying option, letting go to make room for something better. It involves relinquishing old ideas and behaviors to open the way for more appropriate, fulfilling alternatives. While views of sacrifice can have negative connotations implying suffering, we are focused on surrendering those ideas, character traits, and behaviors that hold us back or keep us small. For spiritually inspired manifesting, we sacrifice old ideas to allow new possibilities to emerge.

Acceptance & Service: The Dynamic Duo

This powerful pair—Acceptance and Service—catapult us into a realm of tremendous possibilities. Acceptance dissolves all resistance;

by accepting the presenting reality of any situation, all opposition is neutralized. Add to this the consciousness of service: seeking to give rather than to get, to contribute rather than to take, to participate and join the flow of life rather than sit on the sidelines and simply observe. Service moves us through our weaknesses, beyond our limitations, to a realm of unlimited possibilities. Our involvement in service dislodges our fears, self-doubts, and concerns, and fuels our passage into expressing the best of who we are.

The New Age view of service differs from past views, which associated it with martyrdom—giving to others to our detriment and offering what we thought others needed rather than what we wanted to provide. In this era, our service is transformational because we give what nurtures us while we provide for others. Let this be your guiding question: "What can I give that nurtures and sustains me?"

Guidelines for Inspired Manifesting

Understanding how to make empowering conscious choices makes a significant difference in the quality of our experience. Let's explore some ideas that will propel us toward making conscious, uplifting choices.

Empowering choices assume that Life is "for" us and not "against" us. They assume our human imperfection without any negative judgments. In fact, we intend to enhance our usefulness even with our imperfections. Conscious choices move us away from isolation and guide us toward community. Here are some power questions for making empowering choices:

- Does this give me energy and invigorate me?

- Does this exhaust and deplete me?

- Do I feel loving or loved even as I just
  begin to act on this choice?

Now let's talk about fear. Because we all experience it, there must be some value to it. I have noticed that when I consider fear to be a friend (not my enemy), I begin to recognize how it helps me. Fear signals that my timing may be off or that an idea is not good for me; perhaps something is untrue or impure. Maybe I am not sufficiently prepared and need to get to work! Instead of ignoring it, I get curious: How can fear support my growth?

And it may be time to grow some trust in our honest human effort, dedication, commitment, and discipline. Even when we feel inspired, we can bring awareness to our finite fallibility. Trust develops *through* action, never before taking action. Notice where you place your trust and why. I am aware that I am more afraid when I rely on myself alone, which makes good sense. As humans, we are naturally limited, so it is wise to place our trust in a power source greater than ourselves—and there are many! Place your trust in the Ultimate Reality for inspiration, guidance, and wisdom, and then trust in your humanity to execute the vision. We exist in a co-creative relationship: when I rely on the Universe/God, understanding that I am an agent for Light and Love, I can relax and proceed. This is the ultimate spiritual paradox in action: we are both infinite and finite, limited and unlimited.

Here are a few spiritual guidelines for making inspired choices. How we experience the process is how we experience the result. When we enjoy the process, we will enjoy the result; if we are miserable, we will be unhappy with the result. Remember that we cannot suffer our way into happiness; it is an energetic impossibility. We cannot be happy with what we do not want. Equally, we are always happy with what we truly want. Be honest about what you want—and recognize that people who love us want things they desire for us, which are not always what we prefer for ourselves. We always have enough of what we need to express our Soul's Purposes today; that is how Life is organized. We usually do not have everything for the end result, but we always have enough for today.

Resources always arrive on time when we need them, never too early, never too late. Many of us suffer from financial anxiety. Staying out of financial fear will protect your creativity and integrity. Financial fear corrupts creativity. Avoid it like the plague! Finally, the actions we take today deliver us to the next logical step on our journey. Action is magical. Experimentation is the avenue of expanding awareness. Thinking is a starting point; here on Earth, we must act. By taking action, even small steps, the path opens up to us. If you are anxious, take baby steps. All action is cumulative, supporting our quest.

Do you feel the expansion of consciousness? It's time to open your Records to initiate conscious manifesting. How exciting!

EMPOWERMENT EXERCISE #49
Initiating Conscious Manifesting

Open your Records using the Pathway Prayer Process. Settle into the sacred space that is your Records. Invite the company of your MTLOs. The purpose of this co-creative relationship is to empower you to bring your Soul's Purposes to life in this lifetime. While they cannot "do it" for you or interfere with the natural laws of planetary Life, like gravity and time, they can certainly assist with your understanding of the most efficient and effective ways to experience and express your deepest desires at this time.

Take a moment to review what you hope to manifest: a spouse, a career, improved health, etc.. Describe to your MTLOs what you hope to demonstrate. Share with them as if you were in the company of your most loving, understanding, supportive advisors, which they are. Level One of this type of reading is the story of what you want—your dreams, hopes, and wishes.

Next is Level Two: Causes and Conditions. In this reading, look to see whether you are in a state of unconditional acceptance about yourself and your life. If not, what or who do you want to change? Recalling that acceptance is the foundation of powerful manifesting, ask your MTLOs to help you accept your life exactly the way it is, as if it is supposed to be this way, even if for some reason you may not understand. Ask yourself if it is alright with you to be exactly the way you are right now. Is it acceptable to you to have your life be just the way it is at this moment in time? Imagine that the way things are will not change. Can you allow that to be the case? Imagine that this is exactly the best way for you to be, and your life is perfect "as is," even if you do not understand its perfection.

Next is Level Three; Soul-Level Truths. Given that you are a mere mortal living an ordinary human existence, what can you offer to others or to Life that ignites loving emotions within you? What activities can you participate in that strengthen your experience of love and goodness within yourself? Finally, what makes you feel really good about yourself?

True spiritual service nurtures the giver. What can you contribute; how can you give to others at this point in time, with the resources and skills you have today? What expressions of love can you extend to nurture and sustain you to enjoy all the love within you? What can you do today to feel and enjoy the infinite love within you? In what ways can you extend yourself to others to unleash the love within you, causing you to feel loved, inspired, and fulfilled?

By now, you have a sense of some options for moving forward on your path. Considering the actions that seem appropriate right now, let's take a quick look to see if they are inspired for your ultimate good. Does the very idea of these options give you energy? Or do you feel tired? Are you looking forward to taking these actions? Your human well-being and happiness are requirements for manifesting your Destiny. Therefore, it is wise to take your happiness seriously. Make any necessary adjustments to your ideas to ensure your fulfillment.

And so, for now, leave this be, close your Records by reading the Closing Prayer. Pause to make some notes.

PAUSE FOR SELF-REFLECTION

We have covered some truly exciting territory in this segment of our work! Notice which new ideas appeal to you and which new questions inspire you. I recommend that you take a break now to give yourself a chance to synthesize your understanding. Give yourself a chance to get grounded by eating something delicious, drinking some water, or taking a walk outside in the fresh air. Your dedication to your spiritual awakening is inspiring!

When you are ready to return to this work, we will begin with an exercise designed to ignite awareness of your Akashic Destiny.

EMPOWERMENT EXERCISE #50
Igniting Awareness of Destiny

Open your Records using the Pathway Prayer Process. Give yourself the chance to find the center zone within your Records, a place that is so familiar and reassuring by now—even empowering, enlightening, and remarkably safe. Here you get a sense of the presence of your MTLOs, who are waiting to extend themselves in response to your request for insight, guidance, and wisdom.

One challenge many of us face is accepting the reality of our lives— not as a punishment but as a starting place. Begin with considering acceptance, asking your MTLOs to advise you. Over this series, you have done an amazing amount of work to identify your Soul's Purposes and understand how to manifest them and bring them to life. Recall that our Soul's Purposes are spiritual; they are the physical, material expression of our core spiritual reality. Our Destiny is our inevitable destination; it is built into the permanent part of our Akashic Record. While each of us has our unique dreams, desires, and Destiny, we share a core Destiny in common: to know and love ourselves and others as we are known and loved by the Divine. Our awareness of our Destiny determines the quality of our journey. When we are accepting, the ride is smooth, even when effort is necessary. But if we reject or try to avoid our logical place of arrival, we will suffer because we are in a state of conflict. Awareness of your desire for your destination is the clue that you already have within you the ability to realize your dream. Your Soul's Purposes are how you engage in the world to experience, express, and enjoy the unconditional love within you.

Today, what can you do to unleash more of that love? Allow it to find its way through you so that you can be more satisfied in your life. What can you do to move into your life? How can you conduct yourself to be more involved with the people you love? Let yourself become aware of one action you can take today that will stimulate your journey to manifest more of what you want and less of what you do not want.

And so, for now, we leave this be. Close the Records by reading the Closing Prayer. Pause and make some notes.

The Relationship Between Your Soul's Purposes & Destiny

This is an ideal time to delve deeper into the idea of Inspired Manifestation and to consider the relationship between your Soul's Purposes and your Destiny. Let's begin with this formula:

Desire + Talent + Skill + Action = Inspired Manifestation

These elements occur through us, as us, within ordinary time and place. Each element of this equation is simple and comes naturally to us. When we put them together, the result is Inspired Manifestation. Keep in mind that manifesting is not a singular event. It may seem that way when epic changes appear in surprising ways. Even one-time demonstrations are the product of ongoing developments in consciousness. Manifesting is an ongoing, perpetual occurrence, a fundamental condition of Life. We are always manifesting something. The challenge is manifesting what we want rather than experiences that cause unhappiness.

How are Soul's Purposes related to Destiny? Destiny is part of our Soul's "blueprint," living within us as our completely fulfilled potential. We naturally move toward our ultimate destination and continue to grow into our Destiny because the seed of potential already lives within us. Destiny is the natural consequence of our relationship with the Soul's Purposes and human self, revealed through us as it emerges. When does this happen? Our Destiny is our future vision, potential, possibility, and probability as expressed in the present moment. Our Soul's Purposes always support our ultimate Destiny and act as guides to meaning and fulfillment within each Incarnation.

By increasing our awareness of our human and spiritual selves, we also increase our consciousness of the partnership between our Soul and our human self—and naturally initiate recognition of our Destiny, thereby activating the inner resources we need to achieve our dreams. The core purpose of Destiny is to personally experience and express the infinite love within us through useful service to others in enjoyable, meaningful, fulfilling ways. Our Soul's Purposes are the approach, the path, and the way to the destination: our Destiny. Soul's Purposes are the spiritual essence of Destiny, infused in every action necessary to complete our Destiny. Our Soul's Purposes are the bricks building the path of our Destiny, serving as our governing perspective, our dominant point of view, within each lifetime.

By now, you know what's coming. Let's do an exercise in your Records.

EMPOWERMENT EXERCISE #51
Activating Perpetual Akashic Manifesting

Open your Records with the Pathway Prayer Process. Settle in with your MTLOs into the region of your Records that is familiar, safe, and pure—where you are always welcome. Your trusted spiritual advisors are aware of your sincere desires to manifest your loving Soul's Purposes in this lifetime and discover your personal path of Destiny. Your desires are clues to your natural destination. Your Soul's Purposes are the approach, the path to your destination—the spiritual essence of your Destiny. Soul's Purposes and Destiny work together as partners.

At this time, bring to mind your Soul's Purposes as you understand them. What actions do you take that cause you to experience, express, and enjoy love in this life? Can you understand that this question can propel you on your life path, a journey of activating the infinite love within you, sharing that love with others, and being deeply satisfied in the process, even when it gets difficult? Where will this path of awareness and action lead?

Continuing along this avenue of love and service, where are you likely to arrive? Ask your MTLOs to help you identify this. Get a sense of your Destiny—that combination of your Soul's Purposes and humanity carrying you through this lifetime. Notice where it takes you. Consider that your awareness, experience, and expression of your Soul's Purposes lead you somewhere. They are not the destination but the path you travel. This may change your idea of Soul's Purposes. Ask your MTLOs to help you get a sense of what it could be like for you to live from the place of your Soul's Purposes, rather than considering them a goal or acquisition. Imagine seeking to infuse your activities with your Purposes every day, rather than thinking of them as the result of your activities. How does this affect the quality of your journey?

Now, expand your understanding of manifesting. You are an infinite, eternal, immortal being destined to continually manifest throughout your entire life. With your Soul's Purposes as your guide, you are always in the process of demonstrating your Purposes. The greater your awareness of what ignites the experience of unconditional love within you, the stronger the experience becomes. Using your imagination, sense yourself growing from one manifestation to the next, one demonstration or realization to an even greater one, each following another. The path before you continually expands, enriching and returning to you all the qualities of love and fulfillment as you make your way through your life.

And so, for now, we leave this be and close the Records, pausing to make some notes.

Strategies for Success

Spiritual Law tells us that we can only be successful when we recognize our desired outcome to be good for us, beneficial, fitting, correct, and not harmful in any way. This requires that we have a solid understanding of the positive value and benefits of our goals to realize them. It is a worthy exercise to deliberately identify how our intended manifestations will support us. This practice accelerates our journey to fulfillment. Further, you are the only one who decides what success is for you. Your opinions about successfully manifesting your Soul's Purposes are the only ones that matter. And they are naturally based on your values and talents and evolve as you grow through life.

Our failing is not a moral issue or indication of unworthiness. Rather, it is an opportunity to love ourselves unconditionally, readjust our dreams, improve our skills, and move on. One of the greatest spiritual challenges we all face is how to treat ourselves with kindness and respect even when we do not live up to our own standards.

From an Akashic point of view, sabotage—especially self-sabotage—becomes obsolete. A radical and fascinating idea, sabotage is subversion, something geared to destroy our goal. It may be overt or covert, enacted by us or another. In practice, it is simply evidence that we do not yet believe that what we want is beneficial for us. While it may be harmful, self-sabotage is a way of protecting ourselves. Worry not! As our conviction in the positive value of our manifestation takes root within us, our need to push our good away dissolves, and sabotage ceases to be a problem.

Here are some helpful **Strategies for Success**:

1 Begin where you are.

2 Take one baby step at a time.

3 Do what you can do now with what you already have.

4 Get assistance from people who can help.

5 Know it will take longer than you think: what takes two seconds to imagine may take more than two years to manifest!

6 You will make mistakes, so the question becomes: "What mistakes can you live with?"

7 Do not quit—keep going. It is virtually impossible to completely quit when dealing with Soul's Purposes. Sometimes, we need a break. But even when we think we are throwing in the towel forever, there is no quitting when our Soul's Purposes are at stake.

What about endless challenges, hardships, and obstructionists? Humility tells us not to be surprised by these common elements on our journey. The turbo-charged healing question is always: "*How do I love myself even though* _____?" This idea can catapult us out of the worst situations and ease our passage when things get stormy. Use it often; it helps. The more we can focus and act on our Soul's Purposes as we understand them, the less devastated we are by unfortunate events. At some point, the obstacle will recede, or your relationship with the obstacle will transform. Given that the world is imperfect, we must explore the reality of perfect manifesting in the imperfect world in which we reside.

Let's explore this topic in our Records.

EMPOWERMENT EXERCISE #52
Dealing with Obstructions to Manifesting

Open your Records using the Pathway Prayer Process. Consciously connect with your MTLOs.

By now, you have a pretty good idea of what some of your Soul's Purposes are. Describe which one is most important to you at this time. Bring to mind all the efforts you have invested in this project—all the learning, growing, time, money, etc.

Now, recall a serious obstruction, perhaps an individual or a group who really does not want you involved. Perhaps circumstances keep falling apart, unraveling, or spinning out of control. Describe what happens, the behavior of others—what they do or do not do—that interferes with your success. Describe what happens to you, how you react, and your actions to stop the problem.

Notice that even though it has not been clear sailing, you are still involved in manifesting this ideal. Now, ask your MTLOs to give you some visionary insight into how you can keep going even if the obstructionists never stop their nonsense. Ask yourself: Am I willing to love myself even if this is not easy? Even if I face opposition?

And so, for now, we leave this be and close the Records. Pause to make notes.

Seven Steps to Spiritual Success

You began this spiritual adventure sparked by an internal prompting for more—more aliveness, awareness, and appreciation—seeking to amplify the attributes of love as tangible proof of your spiritual growth and development. Are you beginning to recognize the power of Akashic Light as it illuminates your way, magnifying the Truth of the perpetual presence of light, love, and goodness, no matter what contrary evidence suggests? You are becoming a seeker—and a finder—of the Light. Take your rightful place as part of the solution for the transformation of awareness of humanity, transcending religions, cultures, nations, races, and any other false barriers disguising our oneness. We simply cannot contain the infinite compassion, understanding, patience, and appreciation we have for ourselves and every other human being in creation.

On our way to Inspired Manifesting, the next phase of our development is to reflect on the Seven Steps for Spiritual Success as we begin to tease out our present state of growth, our ideals, and the world in which we live. Our Soul's Purposes and Destiny always involve all three elements. Let's map out the path ahead with these in mind and see what is likely for us in this Incarnation. It is bound to be good!

The Seven Steps to Bring Your Soul's Purposes to Life as revealed to me in my Records are:

1 Awareness
2 Acceptance
3 Appreciation
4 Action
5 Assessment
6 Adjustment
7 Allow & Enjoy!

These seven steps can be applied to any dream in your heart. Use them as your spiritual map to fulfillment of your Soul's Purposes. Let's consider each step to discover deeper Truths, keeping in mind three components: present conditions, ideals, and the world in which we find ourselves.

EMPOWERMENT EXERCISE #53

Applying the Seven Steps to Spiritual Success

Open your Records using the Prayer. Settle in with your MTLOs. Apply each of the seven steps with the following questions:

1 **Awareness.** What am I aware of as my Soul's Purposes? What are my dreams or ideals? And what is the connection between my desire and the world as it is at this time?

2 **Acceptance.** No judgment here. Simply acceptance, allowing my dreams to exist as they are. Am I accepting of my desires and their highest possibilities? And can I accept Life just the way it is?

3 **Appreciation.** Do I cherish and revel in the wonders of my Soul's Purposes and the condition of my consciousness at this time? Do I have a sense of safeguarding the preciousness of my Soul's Purposes? Can I embrace a spirit of wonder when considering the world as it is?

4 **Action.** What am I able to do with the resources I have? What is the relationship between my current abilities and my ultimate dreams? How can I take action in the world, given the present state of things?

5 **Assessment.** What are the results of the actions I took? What happened or not? How does this compare to my hopes and desires? How were my actions received in the world?

6 **Adjustment.** Based on what has transpired, what modifications can I make to my dreams and their launch?

What am I able to do now? And, ideally, what would I like to do? What will work in the world in which I live?

7 **Allow & Enjoy!** Step back. Send your dream into the Realm of Engagement—that powerful dimension of life where your heartfelt desires interact with the world. This is an alchemical realm infused with possibility, surprises, and wonder. Let it happen and enjoy the outcome.

Close your Records; pause to make your notes.

Now is time to enter into the sacred space of your Records to explore manifesting your Soul's Purposes. This is truly your Destiny!

EMPOWERMENT EXERCISE #54
Manifesting Your Soul's Purposes

Open your Records using the Pathway Prayer Process. Consciously reconnect with your MTLOs in the sacred sanctuary that is your Records. Take this opportunity to become aware that you are manifesting your Soul's Purposes right now, arriving at your destination, your Destiny.

Ask your MTLOs to help you become aware of yourself as the intersecting zone of Heaven and Earth. The person you are is the result of an ever-expanding, ever-strengthening partnership between your Soul and your human self. Your dedication and recognition of this multidimensional reality stimulate all the inner resources you require to bring your Soul's Purposes to life.

Get a sense of yourself as the human expression of your Soul in partnership with the Divine. You are here with the primary purpose of experiencing, expressing, and enjoying the infinite love within while you are still in human form. You are igniting the unlimited Light and love within yourself for your well-being and the blessing of everyone you encounter, and expressing the unconditional love of the Divine to yourself and every creature in existence.

Now, at this time, recall your more specific Soul's Purposes for this lifetime, the particular ways in which you experience, express, and enjoy love. It is natural to be moved to tears, full of inspiration and Gratitude as this awareness takes hold within you. Allow yourself to stand in the dimension of profound acceptance of who you are and your ultimate potential, deepening into the space of appreciation for who you are—your gifts, talents, and abilities—in addition to the reality of the life you are living.

As a visionary, you may have an exquisite sense of the ultimate good you are here to deliver. The greater challenge is manifesting this powerful Truth in everyday life. Given the reality of human existence, you can only take one step at a time to unleash this experience and expression of love. And it needs to be something you can do today or in the coming week, something you can do with what you have. What could be your next best action to ignite the love within you? As you consider your next Appropriate Action, how do you feel? What do you think? Will you take action?

Find a quiet place inside yourself and let yourself become aware of the relationship between this idea/action, your Soul's Purposes, and your Destiny in this life. Any resources you require to perform this action are already available to you. If you have to go into debt, scale back the action to something you can manage. One idea, one action at a time, you are building the bridge of your Soul's Purposes to your Destiny. Based on the action you take, access your work to this point. Now, you are positioned to make necessary adjustments. Modify your Soul's Purposes to be a perfect fit for the life in which you live.

Know that your MTLOs are proud of you; they love and appreciate you. As you do your part, as only you can, the world becomes a more loving place. This is the opportunity to allow your Soul's Purposes to interact with life in the Realm of Engagement, where wonderful possibilities emerge and come to life. And you can simply enjoy.

By engaging in this process, you will experience, express, and enjoy infinite love, for this is the Divine Will for every member of creation: to discover the Truth that you are loving beyond all measure and are here to share that love. Together, we all bask in an ocean of love and understanding, shining Akashic Light for our own continual illumination, so that other seekers we know and those we will never meet can more easily find their way.

And so, for now, we leave this be and close the Records. Pause to make some notes.

ONWARD

And now, my friend, you've come to the end of this segment of your Amazing Akashic Adventure. We have covered a tremendous amount of material. As in previous lifetimes, everything you are learning in this lifetime is becoming part of you and empowering your fulfillment. Take some time to give yourself a chance to grow into all you have been learning as you become the person you are meant to be. Enjoy who you are and the riches of your expanding consciousness. You are indeed the ideal agent for your Soul's Purposes. There has never been, nor will there ever be, a better steward for the treasures of your Soul.

This work is designed for people like you who desire change, who are compelled to become all they can be—as loving as possible—within each lifetime. As you recognize and accept your current condition of consciousness, honor yourself for the dedication you exhibit on your heroic quest, even as you position yourself for more. Greater unfolding, revelation, and emergence of the riches of your Soul accumulated through your lifetimes is available, right here and now, in your ordinary life.

Completing this segment is an important episode in your journey, so this is an ideal moment to reflect on your progress. Take a few minutes to think back to when you first began. Notice how your connection with your Records has grown—how much more comfortable and adept you've become in this work! Bravo!

Because we are infinite beings on an eternal quest, there is always more to the journey. Each of us is in the middle of an endless sojourn, a journey of perpetual growth and change. While you may be completing a particular chapter, you are amidst an epic story. Your Akashic Record is the story of your Soul's journey as a human throughout many incarnations, as you come to know and love yourself and others in the same way you are unconditionally loved and respected by Life itself.

As you move forward from here, don't be shy about practicing as much as you can. You will continue to get better, helping yourself and others as you improve. Trust that the Universe will send only people you can help. So never worry that you won't be able to help someone; you are sure to find and be found by people looking for your gifts, talents, and abilities. As you go onward from here, please remember:

- Your Soul's Purposes are spiritual.

- Manifesting is your natural state.

- You are already and always in a co-creative relationship with the Divine.

- The purpose of increased spiritual awareness is fulfilling usefulness—not perfection.

- Your personal Soul's Purposes are precisely what the world needs now and they are meaningful and fulfilling for you!

As we conclude this part of the path together, know that you can achieve the object of your Soul's Purposes. Every step you take in that direction accelerates the release of Light and love emanating from you and radiating out to the world. I'll be looking for you along the way, sure to recognize you by the warmth in your presence, a twinkle in your eyes, and the kindness of your actions. If we meet in person, I know we will recognize each other immediately and enjoy our eternal connection, knowing everything is exactly the way it is meant to be. And it is good.

Until then,
Love,
Linda

the
Pathway Prayer *to* Access
the Heart *of the* Akashic Records©

OPENING PRAYER

I

And so we do acknowledge the Forces of Light,
Asking for guidance, direction, and courage to know the Truth
As it is revealed for our highest good and the highest good of
everyone connected to us.

II

Oh Holy Spirit of God,
Protect me from all forms of self-centeredness
And direct my attention to the work at hand.

III

Help me to know (myself/first name of individual being read) in
the Light of the Akashic Records,
To see (myself/first name of individual being read) through the eyes
of the Lords of the Records,
And enable me to share the wisdom and compassion that the
Masters, Teachers, and Loved Ones of (me/first name of
individual being read) have for (me/him/her/them).
The Records are now open.

CLOSING PRAYER

I would like to thank the Masters, Teachers, and Loved Ones for
their love and compassion.
I would like to thank the Lords of the Akashic Records for their
point of view.
And I would like to thank the Holy Spirit of Light for all
knowledge and healing.

The Records are now closed. Amen.
The Records are now closed. Amen.
The Records are now closed. Amen.

ABOUT THE AUTHOR

Linda Howe, a Doctor of Spiritual Studies, is the leading expert and a pioneer in the field of accessing the Akashic Records for personal empowerment and transformation. She is best known for her Pathway Prayer Process to Access the Heart of the Records© and for making this spiritual resource accessible to ordinary seekers. Her work arises from 25+ years of reading and teaching the Akashic Records to students around the world. Learn more at LindaHowe.com.

ACKNOWLEDGMENTS

This Guide is the culmination of three decades of dedicated work in the Akashic Records—a manuscript revealed to meet the needs of our Souls as we maneuver our ordinary human lives. These are experiential teachings for moments along the path when we seek insight, guidance, and wisdom to be in conscious alignment with our Souls.

As with all worthy projects, many hands have been involved, each serving at the perfect time and in the best possible manner. Everyone brought sincere questions, shared struggles, and opened their hearts. It's been extraordinary being accompanied by such an array of blessings.

The individuals who joined me at the beginning of this Amazing Akashic Adventure were unique in their courage and willingness to step out with the spirit of exploration. Those shoring up the middle years will always be remembered for their persistence, determination, and thoroughness—especially for prompting me to continue plumbing the depths of the Records for even more truths. My most recent supporters bring a remarkable enthusiasm and are so beneficial when my excitement wanes, I veer toward overwhelm, or I require stamina from ever-widening circles of engagement as we endeavor to spread this Light to the ends of the Earth.

A bevy of brave souls serves on my "A" Team—including Jean Lachowicz, Susan M. Lucci, Cindy Waldon, Brian Fischer, Rachel Zargo, Garen

Hudson, and Ryan Bell. Thanks to my treasured Certified Teachers, especially those standing strong in the Light of Akashic Leadership virtually—Patty Collinsworth, Amy Mak, Kevin Jackson, Anika Ray, and Debbie Ritter. I am grateful for a great partnership with Sidney Slover and his team at Learn It Live for making our international adventures possible. Our circle continues to widen with the help of remarkable translators: Austin Chen in Chinese, Lada Shabunina in Russian, and Natalia Talayero San Miguel in Spanish.

Fortunately, I can always count on the loving support of loyal friends: John Holland, Cyndi Dale, Dawn Silver, David Pond, Kathleen Martin, Sharon Black, Marc St. Camille, Homa Shojaie, Melissa Blevins, and Anne Horrigan. Some of my dear supporters have passed on, most recently Amy Szczepaniak and Steven Giese. *I love you all!*

Professional support has been so valuable. Thanks to Susan M. Lucci for her sharp editing skills and for matchmaking this project with such skilled and soulful publishers, Catherine Gregory and Nathan Joblin of Modern Wisdom Press.

Special thanks to the love of my life, Lisa, our fabulous son, Michael, and his wife-to-be, Monica. I am deeply grateful to have such a wonderful family.

You all deserve more than "Thanks." It is a powerful but woefully inadequate word for expressing all the gratitude I feel. As we know, it is impossible to bring our Soul's Purposes to life on our own; each of you has made a tremendous contribution to me in a special way. Thank you from the bottom of my heart for sharing this journey with me. It simply would not have been the same without you.

GRATITUDE & A GIFT

My dear students, what an incredible journey we've shared! For me, the only experience I love more than a spiritual quest is a *shared* spiritual quest. And this has been just that. Together we've learned so much about the Akashic Records and ourselves, including our past, present, and future possibilities. It's been rich and rewarding. How wonderful for all of us!

Our time together has been so precious. While it's important to return to our respective lives to practice what we've been learning, staying in touch will be well worth the effort. I hope you will visit me at LindaHowe.com to discover the latest offerings and opportunities for growth and transformation through the Akashic Records. Here, you can find classes for spiritual enrichment and professional certifications that support your work with others.

And, as a special gift just for you, Dear Reader, I want you to have recordings of the Akashic Light Meditations for each of the three Levels of this Guide. To access your free guided meditations, go to: www.lindahowe.com/Akashic-Meditations.

Until we meet again, keep up the good work! Remember that the distinguishing trait of a Lightworker is deliberately seeking and finding the Light in everyone, everywhere—especially when it seems impossible to do so—and always practicing Unconditional Love.

Made in the USA
Coppell, TX
28 November 2023

24935312R00152